Praise for *Writing Together*

"Writing with a group helps writers break out of the isolation of writing alone. *Writing Together* shows you how to use your writing group to help you discover who you are as a writer and to hear your authentic voice. It is a fine and useful book that respects the writing process. It will bring new life and energy to any group of writers working together."
 —Susan Witting Albert, author of *Writing from Life*

"Creative and practical, *Writing Together* is a wise and inspiring guide on how to establish and sustain a writing group that is a supportive circle and a nurturing laboratory in which to evolve as a writer and as a person."
 —Bonni Goldberg, author of *Room to Write: Daily Invitations to a Writer's Life*

"Much has been written about the solitary work of writers: the isolation seemingly required in order to nurture the creative process, the exile that fosters aesthetic under the austere demands of the muse. But in *Writing Together,* a map is lovingly drawn by which a writer may find her way home again. This is a book not only about writing, but about building community, a guide that sheds a great deal of light on the nature and purpose of coming together for common cause—to speak up and encourage as well as constructively critique, to write honestly, with heart, and most importantly, to keep writing in the solitude with the knowledge that there is a circle to return to, a place where the writer can come in from the cold and be heard."
 —Alison Moore, author of *Synonym for Love*

Writing Together

How to Transform Your Writing in a Writing Group

Dawn Denham Haines

Susan Newcomer

Jacqueline Raphael

A Perigee Book

A Perigee Book
Published by The Berkley Publishing Group
A member of Penguin Putnam Inc.
200 Madison Avenue
New York, NY 10016

First edition: September 1997

Published simultaneously in Canada.

The Putnam Berkley World Wide Web site address is
http://www.berkley.com

Library of Congress Cataloging-in-Publication Data

Haines, Dawn.
    Writing together : how to transform your writing in a writing
group / Dawn Haines, Susan Newcomer, Jacqueline Raphael.—1st ed.
        p.   cm.
    "A Perigee book."
    Includes bibliographical references and index.
    ISBN 0-399-52338-3
    1. Authorship.   I. Newcomer, Susan.   II. Raphael, Jacqueline.
III. Title.
PN145.H28   1997
808'.02—dc21   96-54845
                                                                      CIP

Printed in the United States of America

10   9   8   7   6   5   4   3   2   1

Contents

Acknowledgments   xi
The Black Hole on the White Page   xiii

1 Why a Writing Group?   1
  Why We Came Together   6
  Why a Writing Group?   7
    Regularly Scheduled Meeting Time 9
    Feedback on Your Writing   9
    Sharing Process   9
    Talking Writing   10
  Why Not a Writing Group?   10

2 Writing Together: The Transformation   12
  The Emergence of the Writing Workshop   14
  What the Theorists Say   15
  How Does Freewriting Help?   19
  What Happens When We Write Together   22
    Collective Energy   23
    The Group As Audience   24

Contents

Risking and Paying Attention   26
Giving Up Intention   28
We Experiment Together   29
Then There Is Silence   30

3 Getting Started   33
It Starts with You   35
Finding Other Group Members   39
The "Right" People for Your Group   40
Artistic Considerations   42
    Differences in Experience and Commitment   42
    Genre Differences   43
    Working with Common Interests   44
Organizational Details   46
    How Many Members?   46
    Adding Members   46
    Gender   47
    Where to Meet   48
    When to Meet and for How Long   49
    Leadership   50
How to Structure Meetings   52
    Preparing for the First Meeting: Being Open   52
    Conducting the First Meeting   54
    The Second, Third, and Fourth Meetings   57
    Writing Together   60
    Response and Discussion   61
    Critiquing Drafts   62

4 Writing Prompts   65
Working with Words   67
    Words   67

Contents

Sentences 71

Impromptu Prompts 74

The Four Elements—Stories in a Shoe
Box 78

The List 82

Magnetic Poetry 85

Working with Imagery 89

A Landscape of Your Soul 90

Cutout Images 95

Dreams 99

Writing from Colors 100

Working with Characters 103

What's in a Name? 104

Extending Writing Together: Collaboration 107

Passing Notebooks 107

Pick-Up Sticks or Spontaneous Sentences 110

Writing Prompts in a Bag 113

A Variation: Writing Each Other's
Characters 117

Choose a New Style 117

Sustaining Longer Works 118

5 Talking Writing: Listening Well,
Critiquing, and Speaking Up 120

Listening Well 123

Informal Responses to Freewriting 124

If You Want to Formally Critique Each
Other's Work 126

When You Are Author 126

When You Are Respondent 127

What Writing Groups Talk About 131

Writer's Block 132

Voice 137

Contents

"How Do I Know What This Piece of
    Writing Is and What Do I Do
    with It?"   139
"How Do I Know I'm a Writer?"   140
Submitting Work and Publishing   142
Experimenting, Talking, and Breaking Old
    Habits   144

**6 Sustaining a Writing Group over the
Long Haul**   146
Focus on Writing   148
Attendance   148
    What Attendance Means to Each Writer   148
    What Attendance Means to the Group   151
The Reluctance to Participate   153
    "This Is Like a Class, Isn't It?"   154
    Low Self-Confidence   154
    Fear of Exposure   155
Troubleshooting Critiquing Sessions   156
    The "It's Not Ready Yet" Syndrome   157
    Honesty   158
    Falling into the "Right" vs. "Wrong"
        Mode   159
Jealousy and Competitiveness   160
Leadership Problems   161
Other Interpersonal Issues   163
Family Responsibilities   166
Membership Changes   167
    Gaining Members   168
    Dropping Out   171
Leaving or Ending a Group   172
Staying Open to Change: The Writing
    Retreat   173

Contents

**7 Articles of Faith: The Writing Life Beyond
the Writing Group**   182

Working with Group Prompts   183

Using Readers' Critiques   186

Bringing the Group Back Home   187

Taking Notes   189

A Writing Partner   192

Read! Read! Read!   192

Classes and Workshops   194

Sending Work Out   195

Sustaining the Writing Life   199

Guide to Group Exercises   201

Good Books for Writers   203

Index   215

To the members of our writing group,
with respect

Acknowledgments

From the beginning we received warmth and encouragement from the members of our writing group: Beth Alvarado, Jo Anne Behling, Daphne Desser, Nicola Freegard, Mary Kae MacKenzie, Jackie Newlove, Susan Roberts, and Diza Sauers. We would also like to thank Sandra Florence for bringing us together. This book, and its many ideas about writing and collaboration, would not, of course, exist without them.

Martha Moutray looked at our original proposal and encouraged us to follow our vision. Sheila Tobias shared with us her tireless enthusiasm for writing. Our book has prospered from her uncompromising knowledge of craft. Tilly Warnock, Judith McDaniel, and the members of our group also read earlier versions and offered valuable insight.

Our agent, Judith Riven, has believed in this project from the beginning, and our editor, Sheila Curry, has worked hard to see it to completion. Their professional expertise has made writing this book a pleasure.

Finally, as a working trio, we would like to thank

Acknowledgments

Brian Haines and Lynn Dodson for their dinners, errands, and good humor, and Jefferson Bailey for his generosity.

Dawn Denham Haines thanks her family, sisters Debbie and Dianna, and parents, Carol and Richard Denham. Special thanks to Jan DeGaetani for teaching me to be a student of myself, Steven J. Danenberg for my first teaching job, Eddie Green Scalzo and Jackie Newlove for their good counsel and unflinching support, Anne Deane for her fierce commitment and encouragement, and Brian, for Sam, for laughter, and for dreams fulfilled.

Susan Newcomer would like to thank her mother, Doris, and sister, Nancy, for their endless kindness and generosity of spirit. Thanks also to my other family—Anne Bowen, Chris Bondante, Jefferson Bailey, and Richard Steen—for love and laughter when it mattered. Thanks to Francia White, whose friendship has graced my life for twenty-five years; Selma Rudnick, my dearest writing friend; and Una Ellman and Karen Hill for their good counsel. Special thanks to my daughter Miriam for her feisty sense of self, and finally, to Susan O'Shea, for her fierce attachment.

Jacqueline Raphael would like to thank her parents, Michael and Ruth Raphael, for their love and support, and Lynn Dodson for her encouragement.

The Black Hole on the
White Page

We have stared into it for years, felt its attraction, resisted its pull, fingered its sharp, slick, slippery edge. Every writer in the world has felt trepidation as he or she looked over an empty page, or rather, peered into an empty page, though for most writers, the page is not empty. That is the struggle. It holds shadows, whispers, images, words.

Often, that is exactly why we write. To bring flesh to those fleeting imaginings. But they also hold terror. The terror of memory, the fear of failure, the dance of words and meaning just beyond our outstretched ability to hold them to our hearts.

We stare into a black hole in our universe and then enter it alone. Even an astronaut has connections to Earth as he or she plunges into deepest space. No astronaut peers into the black abyss alone. This solo journey is reserved for the artist, the creator, the writer.

As our group quiets to write, we each bend over our notebooks. Susan N.'s is spiral and the direction is down, she reports, for she bends over not only a notebook, but a darkness in her soul. We all do on occasion. Around the edge we may see shooting stars or planets brimming with life or death, but always in the center is the hole of isolation. We each create alone. We each gather our moods, our memories, our most cherished fears and dreaded successes and flesh them out for all the world to see.

Writing is a lonely task, but what we each discover in the group is that we do not write alone. T. S. Eliot said we create poetry out of other poems. Virginia Woolf said women write out of their mothers. All writers carry a community of writers in their hearts.

But beyond our consciousness and reverence for other writers, our mentors and mothers, are our colleagues and peers, writing right beside us. On any Friday evening we may be musing on the fourth chapter of a favorite author's second book—we carry those words in our hearts, too—but mostly we are moved by the women writing next to us.

What we have found is that all of us bring trepidation to our work. Writing wouldn't be an art if it didn't come from some untamed place inside us. Every member of the group has felt—at least some of the time—embarrassed, alone, out of place. This is a startling discovery for a writer, both humbling and miraculous. We are not alone in our separation.

This is what a writing group offers us: not simply advice on adverbs and adjectives, but the opportunity to face our creative demons side by side, knowing that although the demons are different for each of us, we all have them. And together, we can keep the beasts at bay.

Why a writing group? Because in a writing group a writer comes to trust his or her own voice speaking freely. The beasts lie down and listen, the black hole contracts, the white page shimmers before us like a dove in morning.

Writing Together describes how the eight of us came together and fashioned a writing group to meet our needs. At first, meeting for two hours twice a month, the group simply gave us protected writing time, time that each of us had trouble finding in her life. From simple protected time, during which we wrote together on a common word or theme, we moved on to common story elements, soulscapes, found language, shared narratives, and worked with images and named characters. Frequently we gave feedback on each other's work, and always we talked. These exchanges and exercises pushed our writing skills. We stretched and reached and stretched again. Often we came back with our hands full.

To describe our writing group for this book, the three of us relied on contributions from all our group members. We used our own experiences and those from individual essays written by each member about the group. We also collected writing done in the group over the first two years, interviewed members, and circulated a draft of the book for their comments. We spent long hours remembering, refining, and sifting through our records, both mental and written, about the group's life.

The result is a record of the writing group we began in Tucson, Arizona, over three years ago, a group that has brought us closer to the place in each of us that creates the language of our lives. It is also a guide to the potential of any writing group, of the special transformation that may occur there, and how that transformation is available to everyone who writes seriously.

1   Why a Writing Group?

The task was to change intellectual passion to physical energy and some sort of narrative mastery, from a standing start.

—Annie Dillard
The Writing Life

It's Friday night and we've all had coffee, salsa, and chips. A plate of Pepperidge Farm Orange Milano cookies rests precariously on the edge of the table. Eight of us sit in a circle of futons, wicker rockers, stiff dining room chairs, or on the floor. We are already into our forty-five-minute freewrite (quick spontaneous writing that we do on the spot, unedited and uncensored). We are using four elements in our writing: a railroad trestle, a Cambodian refugee, a fight in a video store, and a ballpoint pen. We pulled the words and phrases from envelopes we made months ago—one envelope each for place, character, situation, and object—which we carry from meeting to meeting. Pens drive across pages and pages of notebooks, journals, and art pads. We rarely stop, all of us accepting the same challenge that we chant over and over to our students: keep your pens moving, no matter what happens. Go with your gut.

We have no timer, no bell that tells us to stop, although eventually someone calls, "That's forty-five." We all adhere to an internal clock, and almost simultaneously pens lift, postures shift, the final word is put in place. When we finish, we don't talk but yawn, stretch, sigh, and one by one stand up, pour more coffee, take another Orange Milano, and respectfully wait for the last of us to bring her work to a close. We ready ourselves to listen.

Dawn has written about a family driving around Washington, D.C., the day before Christmas, showing the capital to a young refugee from Cambodia. She reads in part:

> Mom wanted to take her to the national green-house, filled with poinsettias, large and tiny, their potbellies wrapped in crisp, shiny bows of gold and red. I got more and more annoyed with every mile we drove. I didn't know what to say, what to think, when the girl, at my mother's request, tried to tell us in her choppy English how she, alone and unarmed, escaped from Cambodia on foot. The girl, it seemed, had run and walked without shoes or food to reach the border and cross to safety. And this she told with a huge grin slicing the two halves of her round face. She's shell-shocked, I thought, she doesn't know what she's saying.

When the train trestle appears, it becomes a metaphor for the distance between the two worlds (which sponta-neously connect in the car) and the distance between the family members. The scene ends with the narrator in the backseat, watching two people in a video store mouthing angry words she can't hear.

We assume the narrator is Dawn herself, that she's written from her own experience, and she tells us this is true. We are surprised by how neatly the elements fit Dawn's memory of escorting a young Cambodian woman around Washington, D.C., and how clearly she captures the feelings of a moment fifteen years ago. The elements carry her into fiction, where she explores the dislocation of the people in the car.

Susan R. has written about Thiun, a sixteen-year-old boy who came to the United States at the request of his sister, who had left Cambodia—been "rescued" by the church—eleven years before. She reads in part:

> The day he left Cambodia was so sad. His grand-parents hugged him with the tight embrace of people who knew they would be dead before he'd be able to return for a visit. They had raised him and told him about his parents, the mother and father killed when he was so young. Where had they gone? he had asked. Their bones went underground, they said, with the bones of all the others. Do not think of them, they said. They would want you to go. Go to America. Become a doctor or a big businessman. Make them proud of you.
>
> The letter was in awkward, rusty Cambodian, with crossouts over some words. Obviously, his sister had had somebody help her write it. He could live with her, the letter said, in her trailer. The park was near the train trestle, but it was a friendly place. Lots of Cambodians and Vietnamese lived there. Trailer. This word mystified him. Nowhere in the reruns of *Dallas* had anyone lived in a trailer. What's a trailer? he asked his grandparents. But they didn't know, either.

Writing Together

Susan has written a graceful narrative in the soft, natural voice we have come to value from her.

As Beth often does, she begins her piece with an image she has spotted in the room:

> There is a carved fish on the piano. Its face is red and it has a round black eye. Painted on its black side is an ocean scene. The sprays of water are white, like thin spring lilies. Behind the carved fish is a black-and-white photograph of a train trestle high over a gorge in Colorado. It's a narrow gauge track, one of the few left in the world. I remember when I was a young girl at church camp in Telluride, we used to walk along the trestle, the water of the river ran white below us, the mountainside was green and lush.

At the camp was a Cambodian counselor, exotic with her straight black hair and cigarettes, who describes a dream in which her mother is bathing in an old wooden washtub, naked, in the middle of the street. People ride by on bicycles, and the girl tells her mother to cover herself. The counselor continues,

> "I took a towel to her and began to wrap it around her shoulders. And then, in my dream, I woke up." She flicked the cigarette down into the river. "I woke up and I thought, my mother is dead and I didn't even ask her how she was, I didn't even tell her I loved her."

Beth has gone from an image in the room to a setting from her own life, infused with an adolescent's attraction to an older girl's mysterious presence.

Why a Writing Group?

It is Susan N.'s turn. She reads a short portrait of Sylvia from New York City, now camped under a western railroad trestle, writing about her life in New York,

> about street life, the hucksters, the school children, the purple-haired punks in the East Village and the silky black-haired refugees in Chinatown— Cambodian, Vietnamese, Laotian. These people ran through Sylvia's stories like the cars of the Burlington Northern: uniform, opaque, speeding, so that story after story accumulated a string of characters so similar, a series of events so predictable, that one wondered why Sylvia bothered to write them at all, how she could miss the smell of diesel fumes in the mountain air, how she could disregard the thundering of the train or the popping of the trestle, how she could populate her ragged determined mind with so little of the country around her.

Susan has slipped a kind of self-criticism into her writing, allowing Sylvia to take the rap for her own perceived failings.

We listen to how each of us has blended the four elements into our own stories, nodding, wincing, smiling, and laughing until all are finished. Then we close our notebooks, take more food, talk about our stories and our writing until it is time to go. We say our good-byes and wander out into the alley under a jet-black Tucson winter sky pierced with stars. Once again we have done well at something we do best: not, as one might think, write brilliant prose about unusual characters, but simply come together as a group to write, discovering more about each other and ourselves, growing as writers and

5

friends, continuing the commitment to ourselves, each other, and the necessary act of writing.

Why We Came Together

Our writing group first came together in January 1993. Each of us knew the others as writers and teachers, but we hadn't shared this aspect of our lives. Of the eight of us, some had been in other groups. Most of us had published poetry, short stories, and nonfiction pieces. All of us wrote regularly, but for some reason we were dissatisfied with our writing and with our writing lives.

We were no strangers to discipline and hard work. Many of us had been in academic writing or literature programs or were teaching writing at the University of Arizona. We were women in our thirties and forties; five of us had partners, four of us had children. We shared a lifetime commitment to language and writing, but we wanted something more in the everyday practice of our craft.

Some of us who had been in academic writing programs had found certain criticisms of our work unhelpful and, in some cases, destructive. Moreover, in our attempt to hone craft, many of us felt our advanced degrees had made us self-conscious and mechanical in our writing. Although most of us were accomplished in our craft, we sometimes felt our writing lacked power. In coming together as a group we were seeking a way back to our inner springs, to the passion of our own voices, language, and insight.

Several of us were ambivalent about joining a writing group. We wanted to share our work and develop as writers, but we didn't want the excessive criticism and theorizing we associated with school. Some of us were writing too guardedly. It was time, if we were going to take our writing to another level, to leave the protection and privacy of our work areas and find a greater audience, a greater resonance for our words.

All of us welcomed the chance to meet other writers, to find the camaraderie and support lacking in our academic programs or private writing lives. We also welcomed the chance simply to talk about what was dearest to us—writing. One member especially looked forward to discussing "the small decisions writers make in the everyday practice of their craft."

Each of us was seeking to gain a better understanding of her writing self. Ultimately, we all wanted to be more effective in our writing and to be more responsible, and more responsive, to our talent.

For all these reasons, on a rainy night in January we each settled into our first meeting with hope, fear, and car keys nearby. Writing was, after all, something we cared about greatly, and we hardly knew the other women with whom we'd be sharing something so important. A getaway would be embarrassing, but quick.

But we stayed. Over three years our reasons for continuing in the writing group have changed, but one thing is constant: a writing group, especially one that writes and reads together as we do, encourages, enlivens, and emboldens each of us in ways we never anticipated. Our group has transformed our writing, our relationship to writing, and each of us as writers.

Why a Writing Group?

In *Voice Lessons: On Becoming a (Woman) Writer*, Nancy Mairs describes how a small group of women poets who shared their work at Skimmilk Farm in New Hampshire benefited from their regular meetings:

> And really, what more can we—as writers, as artists, as human beings—do for one another? In the middle of a sentence I'm having trouble with, when my attention strays and I find myself cringing in anticipation of the next inevitable *yech* (and I do cringe; old habits die hard), I say: Let the masters of the written word cling to their bodiless principles. Let them pronounce what is interesting and what is not, what is a poem and what is not, what merits their grudging praise and what does not. For myself, I want another model, I want to hear *this* poem by *this* person on *this* muggy August morning under the pear trees. I want to know what it is doing in the life of her work, and in my life as well. I want to give her the courage to say the next hard thing, without fear of ridicule or expulsion if she strays across the borders of good taste, good sense, or good judgment demarcated by a tradition she has had no part in forming. I want her to do the same for me.
>
> This is what we can *all* do to nourish and strengthen one another: listen to one another very hard, ask hard questions, too, send one another away to work again, and laugh in all the right places.

You also will come to cherish this sense of audience and having a group of trusted and compassionate colleagues with whom you read and write. But you will cherish the group for other reasons as well.

Why a Writing Group?

Regularly Scheduled Meeting Time

Showing up in a group reinforces your commitment to yourself and to your writing. No longer will your desire to write float out there somewhere like a promise you never keep, a promise to write when the dinner is made, the dishes are done, the house repainted, the children grown. If you decide to join a writing group, you have decided to take your writing seriously, whatever that means. (You don't have to know what it means. The process will show you, and you will learn.) Joining or starting a writing group is the first step.

Feedback on Your Writing

In a writing group you can get feedback on your writing and, as we do in our group, undertake impromptu writing together. A writing group is about writing—sharing your work with other writers, having other writers respond to your work, getting the chance to respond to their work, and listening regularly to good conversation about writing.

Sharing Process

Hearing how other writers *go about* writing emphasizes process over product, often overlooked in traditional workshops and academic settings. The final piece of writing, the final period on the final page, is important, but equally important is how the writer arrived at that point: how did she know what she wanted to write about, how did she begin, dig deeper, keep going? What distrust and discouragement did she face and how did she overcome them? How did she manage to put it all together and bring her work to a close? Writers spend more time in the *act* of writing than in the appreciation of a finished piece of work. We all have a lot to share and learn about each other's writing process.

Talking Writing

Also beneficial is to hear other people speak about their writing; to talk about voice, character, plot, and writer's block; to learn how other people submit work for publication; and about classes and workshops, readings and bookstores. The writing life is less intimidating if knowledge is shared.

Why Not a Writing Group?

For all the reasons why you might consider joining or forming a writing group, however, here are some reasons why you should *not* join a writing group.

- Don't join a writing group if you expect to be told how to become a great writer.
- Don't join a writing group if you expect to be told you *are* a great writer.
- Don't join a writing group to get published, get famous, or get rich.
- Don't join a writing group to avoid the traditional standards of clear, rigorous writing.
- Don't join a writing group if you want help with adjectives, nouns, verbs, or adverbs, or at least if you think your primary problem with writing involves your use of adjectives, nouns, verbs, or adverbs.
- Don't join a writing group if you know all the answers about writing.

Why a Writing Group?

- Don't join a writing group if you don't have any questions about writing.
- Don't join a writing group if you don't read.
- Don't join a writing group if you can't take criticism.
- Don't join a writing group if you are excessively defensive.
- Don't join a writing group if you are excessively offensive.
- Don't join a writing group if you don't love language.

Do join a writing group—or start one if you can't find one to join!—if you believe in the power of words, if you believe in the power of people's lives and the language they bring to those lives, if you write to make sense of your life, if you stay up late reading, if you get up early to write in your journal, if you make up stories about people you see on the street, if you scribble lines of poetry on scraps of paper and stuff them in your pocket, if you relish the sound of words, if you feel you must write or wither.

A writing group can be your handiwork. Make the effort to form a group that will address your needs, meet your highest expectations, and transform your writing and your writing life. It is a risk well worth taking.

2 Writing Together: The Transformation

> Over any extended period of time, being an artist requires enthusiasm more than discipline. Enthusiasm is not an emotional state. It is a spiritual commitment, a loving surrender to our creative process, a loving recognition of all the creativity around us.
>
> —Julia Cameron
> *The Artist's Way*

Writers flourish not in isolation but in community. Witness the English pub, the American bar, the Algonquin's Round Table, Harlem's Cotton Club, Stein's 27 rue de Fleurus, and Martha's Vineyard. Despite society's romantic view of writers and other artists as tortured, tormented, and isolated, most writers crave companionship, response to their work, and inspiration. Although the act of committing words to paper may be a solitary pursuit, writing is not so much a private act as a personal one, not so much an isolated art as a visionary one. Who better to share the length and breadth of the creative journey than other writers?

The transformation we have experienced in our writing group comes partly from this shared community. Thinkers and writers have always sought companionship. Anne Ruggles Gere, author of *Writing Groups: History, Theory, and Implications*, explains that writing groups in this country emerged out of an American tradition of "mutual improvement" groups. With only two years of formal education, Benjamin Franklin started one of the first mutual improvement groups in 1728. Members met weekly to comment on current events and discuss their written essays. Gere and other social historians find a uniquely American feature in these groups: a democratic view of learning and a tendency for individuals to work together to increase their knowledge and improve their lives.

Over the next 200 years, writing clubs, developing out of this impulse for self-education, provided members with feedback on their short stories and nonfiction papers. Participants were told of the strengths and weaknesses of their writing, as revealed by this critique, quoted by Gere, given to the author of a short story from the Seattle Writers Club, founded in 1903:

> On the positive side, it is interesting, there is some good characterization, the plot is out of the ordinary and therefore salable, and young people would like it, but the opening is too slow, there are too many characters, it does not truly portray the character of American girls, some specific words and phrases don't work, and it is doubtful that there are any motor roads in the Black Forest.

Social and political developments in this country over the last three decades have generated even greater interest in writing groups. The women's movement, for example, has encouraged women to find a "voice" for their experiences, which have often been denied, distorted, or trivialized in the past. "Consciousness-raising" groups from the sixties and seventies allowed women to revise and reevaluate their own experience in the company of other caring and supportive listeners. The Civil Rights, antiwar, New Left, and environmental movements all sustained a consciousness critical of outside authority, encouraging individuals with common interests to come together to work on common problems. A burgeoning interest in the creative process, as well as in spiritualism, growth-consciousness, self-help, and recovery, has continued to encourage individuals to find significance in their lives, often through writing.

The Emergence of the Writing Workshop

Throughout the eighteenth and nineteenth centuries, self-improvement groups tended to meet separately and spontaneously, without benefit of outside authority, in contrast to academic writers' programs, which formalized the practice of giving feedback to writers. In the 1930s, the University of Iowa Writers' Workshop, one of the premier writing workshops in the country, developed a system for training creative writers that dominates academic programs to this day. Writers who have studied or taught at Iowa include Ted Berrigan, Robert Bly, Raymond Carver, John Gardner, Gail Godwin, Jane Howard, John Irving, Donald Justice, Philip Levine, Flannery O'Connor, Jayne Anne Phillips, W. D. Snodgrass, William Stafford, Wallace Stegner, Mark Strand, James Tate, Mona Van Duyn, Dan Wakefield, John Edgar Wideman, and Tennessee Williams. Their success, and the strength of Iowa and other writing programs, have encouraged many writers to seek professional training.

The traditional workshop model focuses on participants' critical readings of each other's work. A writer brings in a draft of an essay, story, or poem and distributes copies to the workshop participants. The participants take the draft home and read and reread it, marking questionable passages or areas to be improved. Their comments may include personal reactions ("I didn't like this part") or larger, more impersonal judgments ("the plot is weak"). In the subsequent meeting, the writer is in the hot seat, urged to remain silent during the critique and provide no information or explanation as to the piece's intention, genesis, or significance so as not to influence comments from others or engage in debate over readers' reactions. In this way, the reading is "pure"—that is, most like how the general reader might receive the work. Participants analyze the work, indicating its strengths but more often its weaknesses, banalities, clichés, and sentimentalities. Often, participants make specific suggestions for revision. This model of critique is thought to bring out the best in a writer, to help him or her hone craft and learn from peers.

Most writing groups follow this model: members share work in progress and receive helpful criticism in return. But despite the obvious benefits of the workshop model, our group has tried to improve on its limitations. An equally important task for us as writers is to encourage the generative part of our writing. We benefit from support and insight when we're just beginning something, even before we know what a piece is about or may become. Also, even more than support for a particular piece of writing, we have found that support for the creative process itself is important to us. An exclusively critical model does not fit our needs, so we have joined criticism with an emphasis on generative writing.

What the Theorists Say

When we first came together, we knew a lot about the formal theories of writing. Most of us teach writing—

either creative writing or composition classes—and most of us have been through undergraduate and graduate programs in writing or literature. We have read Peter Elbow, Donald Murray, Ken Macrorie, and other theorists. We instruct students in generative writing, drafting, revising, editing, and the classic four modes of composition: narration, description, exposition, and argumentation. But when we came together in our writing group, our only interest in theory was how it informed our own writing practice.

Probably the most important insight our writing group members share—with one another and with a host of other writers on the subject—is that the creative process is a two-step affair. Peter Elbow was writing about this in the early seventies, although other recovered and newly reprinted texts, like Dorothea Brande's *Becoming a Writer* and Brenda Ueland's *If You Want to Write*, were recommending the same approach as early as the 1930s.

In *Writing Without Teachers*, published in 1973, Elbow challenges the traditional writing model. For ages, he argues, writing teachers have been telling students first to determine what they want to say, then fashion that meaning in language. In this model, writing is straightforward, logical, and sequential. One shouldn't start writing until after thinking through the purpose of the piece. A muddled result reflects muddled thinking: the writer didn't have a clear enough idea of what he or she intended to write in the first place.

For Elbow, this model is "backwards." Writing is an "organic, developmental process," he believes, one that requires the writer to dive in and write without knowing in advance the point or shape of the piece. Only when the writer is finished is the meaning clear. "Writing is a way to end up thinking something you couldn't have started out thinking," Elbow writes. "What looks inefficient—a rambling process with lots of writing and lots of throwing away—is really efficient since it's the best way you can work up to what you really want to say and how to say it."

Alice G. Brand, a contemporary poet and academic, notes another kind of division: a first draft, she says, begins intellectually or emotionally, driven either by logic or passion. At a later point, in the rewriting, the writer always has the option of "switching gears," moving from the emotional to a cooler, more rational mode of argument, or back again to feeling. Brand faults the academy for telling students they must write in one or the other mode, that they must separate thinking from feeling. When writing students are asked to analyze published poems and stories as models, they are given the wrong impression that they should always *think* their way through their expressive writing, instead of disciplining their feelings with craft.

Sixty years earlier, Brenda Ueland, author of *If You Want to Write*, urged writers to allow their imaginations time for "moodling"—her word for "long, inefficient, happy idling, dawdling and puttering"—especially to get back to writing after skipping a day. Appreciation of idleness contradicts what most of us were taught: that writing requires continual, willful effort. Ueland says when we are writing, we should feel "happy, truthful and free, with that wonderful contented absorption of a child stringing beads in kindergarten."

These thinkers suggest that the writing process involves more than the logical, rational side of our brains. It feeds as well on idle thoughts and earnest passions. This is easier to say than to achieve, because to write creatively, one must concentrate *and* relax. In *Writing with Power*, published in 1981, Elbow elucidates this claim, explaining that "writing calls on two skills that are so different that they usually conflict with each other: creating and criticizing." He continues:

> Most of the time it helps to separate the creating and criticizing processes so they don't interfere with each other: first write freely and uncritically so that you can generate as many words and ideas as possible without worrying whether they are good; then turn around and adopt a critical frame of mind and thoroughly revise what you have written—taking what's good and discarding what isn't and shaping what's left into something strong.

Why is this separation of powers important? Because creativity and criticism work at cross purposes. How many times have you squelched a good idea with the words "it's stupid," "it's banal," "it won't work"? (Criticism of the work can also be turned on the writer: "I'm stupid," "I'm banal," "I can't do this.") Or, while you revise an important paper or story, are you interrupted with completely new ideas or creative approaches to the project? Endorsing this separation of powers, Elbow recommends that you be "loose and accepting as you do fast early writing; then be critically tough-minded as you revise what you have produced." By practicing this two-stage process, he concludes, "You will get practice in the larger skill of moving back and forth between conflicting temperaments so they enhance each other instead of fighting each other."

Writer Gabriele Rico takes an even firmer stand on this point. In *Writing the Natural Way: Using Right-Brain Techniques to Release Your Expressive Powers*, she argues that

18

our "mental makeup" is "two-sided." One side thinks in terms of "the connectedness of things and events"; the other, in terms of "parts and sequences." She goes on to say that recent discoveries in brain research have shown that the left hemisphere or "sign mind" is largely engaged in the rational, logical representation of reality as well as with parts and logical sequences. The right hemisphere or "design mind" thinks in "complex images; it patterns to make designs of whatever it encounters, including language, which, instead of clearcut signs, become *designs* of nonliteral meaning." Rico argues that the two processes are dissimilar because they involve different areas of the brain.

Clearly, our critical minds need to be turned down when we create. If we write out of intention as well as attention, we need to bring as much focus and energy to the activity as possible, without releasing a powerful stream of doubt, self-criticism, and judgment flowing against our will, beneath our consciousness.

How Does Freewriting Help?

In *Writing Without Teachers*, Elbow talks about "fast, early writing," "automatic writing," "babbling," "jabbering," or "freewriting"—simply writing whatever comes into your mind for a set amount of time. "The only requirement," he says, "is that you never stop"— that is, until your time is up.

Because writers tend to edit their writing as they go along—overburdened by the dos and don'ts of correct writing—they edit out not only "bad writing" and "mistakes" but often "unacceptable" thoughts and feelings as well. "Premature editing doesn't just make writing hard," Elbow says. "It also makes writing dead." The point is to mine whatever thoughts and feelings you may have—the unacceptable as well as the acceptable—to discover what you have to say. Later you can go back to rewrite, prune, and polish.

It would seem that the freewriting approach is apt to encourage garbage, in contrast to the generally accepted belief that "real writing" is controlled, correct, contained. However, while freewriting may produce garbage, and it would be wrong only to freewrite and never to be critical or precise, this only confirms our sense that writing is a two-step process, the first part of which is somewhat chaotic, when you give yourself permission to generate material—ideas, insights, snippets, explorations. The second part is critical, when you take that raw material and fashion it according to some—usually—more logical, linear standard.

Our group goes one step further: we have redefined our sense of garbage. Garbage is a kind of judgment we simply do not make anymore. In our writing, we have come to respect whatever words flow onto the page. What we write is what we write, and we learn to accept it for what it is. Sometimes an occasional gem—a turn of phrase, character, scene, description, or insight—sparkles through our hasty, inchoate scribblings. Sometimes not. But sometimes our hasty, inchoate scribblings are as powerful, as coherent and significant, as any writing we have done elsewhere. We see freewriting as a chance to silence our critical mind, a chance to let our deeper insights and more sentient coherence emerge, a chance to find voices more full of meaning than propriety, more full of chance encounters and surprising, fleeting insights than logically assembled, appropriate prose. As our group writes together, the language that emerges often coheres by way of nonlinear association, by way of back-stitched, recursive logic. For us, this is real writing, not garbage at all.

Elbow thinks that writers can be too careless, of course, but not in the way one might think. Carelessness is not a misspelled word, a faulty sentence, a grammatical blunder. True carelessness, he argues, is when the writer fails to give full "attention, focus, or energy" to the activity at hand.

We don't mean to discredit the traditional standards of clear, rigorous writing. In *On Writing Well*, William Zinsser argues for brevity, simplicity, clarity, and humanity in writing. In *The Elements of Style*, E. B. White and William Strunk, Jr., espouse the elementary rules of usage and principles of composition. John Gardner's *The Art of Fiction* and Janet Burroway's *Writing Fiction* are invaluable guides for thinking critically about narrative. Mary Oliver's *The Poetry Handbook* is a thoughtful guide to the craft of poetry. Numerous writers describe how revision allows a writer to "re-envision" a piece of work. It often takes many drafts to clarify an insight or develop an image, idea, character, or scene.

What our group emphasizes, however, is the need for balance, the need to reposition and revalue the first stage of the writing process. Invention and discovery are as important as revision and editing. In our group, we practice the first stage along with the second. Freewriting in our group has expanded our awareness of both parts of the writing process in ways we never imagined.

What Happens When We Write Together

We may agree upon a particular "prompt"—a word, phrase, or premise from which we begin our writing—and agree upon how long to write together, but the process of freewriting is unique for each of us. Jacqueline composes furiously across a medium-sized spiral notebook, pressing her ballpoint pen hard onto the paper, turning pages quickly, filling four, five, six of them with a complete little fiction in less than thirty minutes. Beth and Susan R. both write in large sketchbooks, each page a block of white space without lines to constrain their thoughts. Beth may look up from the page and appear to daydream, but we know from hearing her talk about her writing process that she is seeking images, which is where she likes to start writing. Susan N. writes steadily in her spiral notebook, pauses, writes again purposefully, never giving up on herself or the page, no matter how frustrating or difficult. Daphne comes to the group with her laptop and quietly taps out her prose and poetry.

Our different styles of freewriting from a prompt reflect our different writing processes. Jacqueline bears down on an image or phrase suggested by the prompt and keeps writing until a story emerges. Objects in the room spur Beth to write. Focusing on the grapes in a bowl helps Beth work a story gradually into her freewriting. Susan R. alternates between pure invention and writing from her own experiences, using her "nonfiction voice." Susan N. finds herself starting with an idea, approaching her writing "cerebrally," freewriting fast, and eventually letting her emotions take over.

Writing Together: The Transformation

Discoveries about our writing process follow from the "interior work," as Susan N. calls it, of freewriting. Whether done individually or in a group, freewriting comes from an intensely private place and cuts through "left-brain" thinking to the fresh language of poetry and fiction. By sharing our freewriting, we transform our attitudes toward our own writing and learn about ourselves as writers.

It satisfies us all when we see connections between what we generate in the group and what we are working on outside the group. It's rewarding when sketches for novels, essays, poems, and stories are born in the group. But more significant to our writing lives, we respond to other voices, sounds, and texts; writing in the group, we learn better how to write alone.

Collective Energy

One powerful effect of freewriting together from a prompt is the sense of collective energy we feel in the room as we write. Once we start, the group keeps us writing. Even when we feel discouraged or tired, it's nearly impossible to give up with the others writing beside us.

Susan R. characterizes these first few moments of writing together as a kind of synergy:

Everyone's pen begins to move, but it isn't a threatening, panicky sound, as in a final exam. No, it is the companionable background noise to people thinking, generating their own writing energy, creating an almost palpable buzz or hum in the room. I am drawn up into that force field myself.

Similarly, Nicky describes a power source in the room when we write together:

> Whether or not you are open to experiencing it, the power will feed your desire to improve your skill. The thoughts written in those moments create an energy in the room and create magic for the women who share that moment, each, sitting in a circle, head down and focused, pushing pen across page, reaching inside toward imagination and creation.

Susan N. describes this as a ''force field, a sense of urgency'' as we write together. We are gathered, in fact, to uncover our individual expressions. Focusing collectively and sharing the commitment to keep writing, we create a powerful force that reminds us that as writers, we are not alone.

The Group As Audience

Another advantage of writing together in our group is that our words connect to real people. Every other week, writing together gives us a flesh and blood audience. Most writers share a desire to show someone what is happening in their writing no matter how good or bad they think it is. In the group, our initial writings, no matter how messy or raw, are immediately made public. The value of an audience is not a new discovery. In 1938, in *If You Want to Write*, Brenda Ueland wrote:

> Once I was playing the piano and a musician, overhearing it, said to me: It isn't going anywhere. You must always play to someone—it may be to the river, or God, or to someone who is dead, or

24

to someone in the room, but it must go somewhere.

That is why it helps often, to have an imaginary listener when you are writing, telling a story,
so that you will be interesting and convincing
throughout. . . .

This recognition that art, music, literature is
a sharing, that a live, alternating current is passing
swiftly between teller and listener (even though
imaginary or transcendent) is absolutely essential
in the process, cleared up many things that puz-
zled me.

It is one thing to write from the heart, to imagine
that an audience out there will understand what we
mean. It is quite another to have an audience respond
to our words not three feet from our notebook. As Beth
says, "When you work alone, you may lose the sense of
audience, or you don't have one in your mind anymore,
or it's some abstract one, like the market. When we write
in the group we're no longer working in a vacuum."
Some writers claim to write better when freewriting in
the group than alone at home precisely because they
know they will be reading their piece aloud.

Our group is an ideal audience because each of us
takes the same risk together, and we acknowledge that
freewriting is rough and raw and not to be judged. These
conditions relieve the pressure to write "brilliantly." On
some days we may dive deep into the waters of our subconscious and come up with treasures. On others, we
merely skim the surface. Hearing our freewriting read
aloud no matter how "good" or "bad" helps us better
understand that being a good writer isn't writing *well*
every day, but simply *writing* every day we say we will.

Writing Together

We have much to learn just from reading out loud in the presence of others: how we sound, what in our voice is strong, from where we draw our material. The short declarative sentence acquires new power and precision; the slippery, deferent tone gains majesty; the ring of self-deprecation or sadness takes on a darker meaning. We read aloud as much for the experience of listening to our own language as for feedback.

When we leave, each of us takes home the hum of attention, interest, and compassion. In her private writing time, Dawn remembers what it feels like "to write freely, daringly, and urgently in the group." She has a sense of someone listening, a sense of why she is taking pains with her words. "The audience stays with me," she says.

Risking and Paying Attention

When we dare to expose our raw writing, we break out of isolation and fear. No longer do we bury our work in closets and trunks. Taking this risk together forces us to pay attention to how we put words on the page.

Observing herself as a writer in the group, Dawn began to understand how her writing takes shape:

When I was writing stories for creative writing classes, writing came slowly and awkwardly. I wrote out of memories and from fragments or observations I kept in journals, trying to put them into a prescribed form, a formula. These stories felt false and contrived. But when I learned from the group to write whatever came to my mind in response to the prompt, many of the stories I wanted to tell, the experiences I wanted to explore, emerged in fast, deliberate, detailed freewritings, with more urgency and life to them than my stories. I began to trust that if I simply wrote, no matter what the prompt, something of importance or something worth returning to would surface. The more I wrote freely like this in the group, the more I allowed myself to let the act of writing guide me to the heart of a piece rather than trying to create mechanically correct stories.

Like Dawn, Beth learned from the group to try a new approach to a particular section of her novel in progress. After writing one evening from the prompt "shrines," Beth noticed that her voice trembled as she read aloud. Paying attention to what was happening, she heard and felt the emotion in her writing. Later, when she returned to her novel, she was determined to infuse it with the same emotional power. Reading in front of an audience had given her a new outlook. She says,

> In some mysterious way, writing together has helped me to write with more power. No matter what emerges after that twenty or thirty minutes of freewriting, it's always a map of the process of its own creation. I can see each thread very clearly and that, in itself, helps me to become more conscious and trusting.

Daphne began paying attention to how her immediate emotions inform her poetry when she wrote from the prompt "I kissed a _____ once." She says of that evening,

> Looking back, I don't think my piece could have been written at any other time. The poem came

out of the emotions of being in the group that night. I was feeling some confusion, anger, and pain—all the ways I hadn't been able to connect.

Even if she was unaware of it, Daphne took a risk that night by letting her emotions carry her writing. The result was a moving, lyrical poem (see page 75). When she read it aloud, we sensed how powerful her freewriting experience had been . . . and we could see and hear that reading the poem aloud challenged her further. Daphne's writing that night reminded us of how writing is linked to risk.

Paying attention as we take these risks together helps us locate the source of our strongest prose and poetry. Dawn loves "reading that last sentence, the one I just wrote down, the one that is a little gift, because I don't know where it came from. I like being surprised."

Giving Up Intention

When we freewrite together, we give up the part of ourselves that inhibits our writing. Frequently we can fully mine our experiences in response to the prompts without deciding how or what to write about in advance. Many of us have found this one of the most liberating aspects of writing together. Beth calls this "giving up intention":

A group of unrelated words or someone else's sentence forces you to rely on intuition. You have to give up control, and any illusion of control, and give in to the moment, paying attention even to the way it feels to hold your own pen—how it feels when your own pen stops and the focus shifts from inside your head, the landscape there and its inhabitants. There is, of course, the outer landscape, other pens moving across the page, the birds singing outside, a car revving its motor—these outside elements both intrude *and* help you begin.

By freewriting in the group, Jacqueline discovered that she needed to value her intuitive writing more. Before she joined, she had kept journals full of fragments of raw writing, where she "played with scenes and characters." Although she liked this unstructured freewriting, she didn't consider it "real" writing and never developed it. But once in the group, hearing and feeling the power and emotional strength of her freewriting, she realized that this writing *was* "real" and that she was beginning early drafts of stories and poems. Her freewriting was more relaxed than some of her highly polished stories because she didn't load it up with expectations. Now, she regularly takes home her freewriting from the group and works it into her fiction and poetry.

We Experiment Together

By freewriting together from a prompt, we have created a noncompetitive place for consciously experimenting with our writing. We push each other to take on new challenges in form, plot, style, and voice.

Susan N. writes mostly autobiographical pieces in the group. Writing for her is connected with grief and loss. Watching the others write fiction, however, or write about childhood memories full of humor, pushed Susan N. to explore her memories less judgmentally, with more openness and optimism.

Susan R. and Jacqueline usually write fiction. Their characters, plots, and settings have impressed the others.

Although this writing is satisfying to her, Jacqueline noticed that others wrote autobiographical pieces with an urgency and emotion she envied. From the group she learned she rarely challenged herself to write directly from her own experience, so she decided to try: "It wasn't that I felt I was doing anything wrong. But once the novelty of completely unrestrained, entirely fictitious freewriting wore off, I wanted to explore writing about my life. This decision came partly from listening to the others and feeling the power of their stories."

We undertake these experiments individually, inspired by one another's writing. After hearing Susan R.'s work, Dawn tried writing more fiction. Susan N. also became more confident developing her intricate wordplay. For Daphne, experimentation meant deciding one evening not to work on the short story she was developing through successive freewrites but rather, to follow wherever the prompt took her.

Any one of our prompts may present a challenge and an opportunity for experimenting. Whether we exchange notebooks, borrow lines from each other's texts, or use drawings to write (see chapter 4), we encourage each other to push past our limits.

Then There Is Silence

Writing in the group can be difficult and intimidating, of course. Nicky says her first experience writing together was "not so totally different from sitting naked" in our writing circle.

> I knew I needed to let the words come out, yet I
> felt every boundary in each word falling on my
> tongue while I read my first piece aloud, as if it
> were as thick and pasty as a fresh adobed wall.

Still, the experience was the beginning of an opening, like crossing a chasm toward a better understanding of myself and of my work. The crack opened. I was facing fear and being fearless.

Susan N. has trouble quieting her negative voices, and yet she continues to write in the group, to put herself in an uncomfortable place because she gains something.

Perhaps my exposure to the writing group has made me write more publicly than I was prepared for. If this is true, then I have learned a great deal from the writing group. I have learned what it feels like to do poorly at something I want to do well at more than anything in the world and persevere.

Beth also notices those moments when you look up during a freewrite and see the others writing, when "feelings of inadequacy or competition begin to creep up from your stomach." We all have heard these voices, the ones that say we aren't good enough, fast enough, creative enough, intelligent enough, original enough. We are afraid we won't be able to write anything worthy of reading this night; worse yet, we fear we won't ever produce anything worth reading again. These silencing voices in our heads keep us from being spontaneous and free.

Jo Anne, one of our original members, eventually left the group because she didn't find writing together useful to her writing process. This was different from any way she'd worked in the past. She describes herself as a "heavy reviser" and a "slow writer." For her, writing is an essentially private act, and she doesn't share her work until it is polished. Although she was committed to trying to write in a group, she found herself increasingly plagued by negative inner voices as she watched others around her write quickly and heatedly. In time her doubts defeated the purpose of being in the group, so she left. However, Jo Anne maintains that she benefited from joining and leaving the group. From the experience she learned to value and accept her working style.

We've all struggled with writing in front of others and then reading that writing aloud. We've faced resistance to sharing our raw writing, resistance to an open forum as opposed to the quiet privacy of our own desks where we write and revise and write again. Breaking this isolation can make us feel painfully vulnerable. These responses to writing together should never be ignored. They may be more intense for some than others, but they remind us that it is normal, even necessary, to freeze up occasionally when writing in a group. Such blocks teach us humility and respect for the mystery that takes place whenever, alone or together, we put written words on a page.

Whether members write together or not, joining a writing group formalizes your commitment to yourself as a writer. But writing together further commits you to your *development* as a writer. We are nourished by the group's collective energy, we have come to trust the group's consistency as an audience, we experiment together, and we respect and accept even our occasional silences.

3 Getting Started

You will have to find other acquaintances, persons who, for some mysterious reason, leave you full of energy, feed you with ideas, or, more obscurely still, have the effect of filling you with self-confidence and eagerness to write.

—Dorothea Brande
Becoming a Writer

The five women who attended our first group meeting three years ago had what you might call an extremely "literal" idea of a writing group. We came together at a member's home on a rainy winter night, sat down in a circle, and wrote for twenty minutes in silence, using the word "fathers" as a prompt. We wrote quickly, without editing, and then each woman read her work aloud. Few comments were made about the pieces. After everyone read, we talked about how it had felt to write together.

This simple beginning led to the growth of an important relationship between the eight of us who now belong to that same writing group. We did not know, in the beginning, that this writing group would be special. All of us had put writing squarely at the center of our personal and professional lives, from the fleeting glory of being published to the day-to-day work of writing, editing, or teaching writing at local institutions. The idea of meeting together with other writers was not extraordinary to us.

Writing Together

At the time we formed our group, most of us were getting technical help with our work in workshops or from editors and agents. Yet some of our members were stuck in a writing "rut" (our polite term for a writing "block"), and others were exhausted by the numerous writing workshops they had taken. To explore our range and grow creatively, we envisioned a writing group that did more than give feedback on particular stories, essays and poems; we imagined one that nurtured our overall writing process. The kind of group we sought would give us feedback on *all* aspects of our writing.

Perhaps our considerable classroom experience, as both teachers and students of writing, helped us create a different kind of writing group: we knew what we *didn't* want. Right from the start, we used our meetings to investigate how each writer took a suggested topic or prompt and made it her own, bringing her unique voice, experiences, and creativity to the writing.

We may have groaned the night Beth suggested "desire" as our prompt. It's such an awkward and difficult topic to write about. But our pieces turned out well. In fact, those who had groaned did best of all. Once the group's momentum set in, once we were freely rhapsodizing and creating, we wrote with fervor and zest. All our tiny fictions, prompted by the word "desire," grew out of the challenge of finding our truths despite the fear of exposure.

That's what writing does to you, and it's one way we hope your writing group will transform you: to make you unafraid of writing the truth. Although you may weave and meander and even circumvent the truth, if you are trying to say something real—actually, whenever you're really trying to say anything—the truth often finds you. It takes hold of your pen, forcing you to write it down.

Or, you keep stumbling, day after day, each time you open the page to the troublesome section of your work. And then finally, one day you plunk down the truth, and you either weep out of gratitude because you can proceed to the next chapter of your novel, or you go to the refrigerator for a snack and feel slightly more pleased with the world.

But how do you create a group that will encourage your best work? What do you do at the first meeting? Beginnings—of stories and of relationships—are important. In the first few meetings a new writing group can generate enthusiasm and commitment or lose momentum so rapidly that within weeks it falls apart. Central issues, such as what you want to gain from a writing group, and nitty-gritty organizational details, such as when, where, and how long to meet, can easily turn first meetings into confusing, frustrating affairs.

Our first meetings allowed us to define both ourselves and the workings of our writing group. Whether you're just starting out or belong to a group whose original purpose you've outgrown, you, too, can fashion a writing group that surpasses your initial expectations and transforms your writing.

It Starts with You

A writing group's beginning actually starts before the first meeting, with each writer thinking about what she wants and needs from a group. Maybe you've already started. Perhaps you've visualized an idyllic cafe for your meetings, a stylish literary coterie, and fast friendships. But what will your writing group *do*?

When we ask writers to describe the work of a writing group, they use stock images. "Everyone reads drafts of each other's writing the week before a meeting, then comes in and gives feedback," they say. Or, "It's a class without a teacher." These views are not false, just limited. Maybe you are a fiction writer with two half-finished stories, and in three months you'd like to improve them. You want a writing group's help in determining what does and doesn't work in these stories. But is that *all* you want? Will the exclusive focus on revising feed you at different stages of writing, such as generating material, finding good model writers to read, overcoming writer's block, and submitting your work for publication?

When our group was forming, we worked *against* the format of traditional workshops, in which the primary task is reading one another's drafts and giving feedback on them. In addition to critiquing one another's work, we wanted to be inspired by one another. We wanted our work together to feed our hunger for writing, so that we made the time to work on that poem that kept getting pushed aside while we completed a hundred other tasks. Like members of other writing groups have told us, we wanted to get inside each other's stories and poems. We wanted our characters and stories to come alive in the group.

If you are working alone right now and in search of a group to join or create, take some time to think about your needs as a writer. Ask yourself how serious you are about writing. Do you feel that you are a "real" writer? Are you afraid of sharing your work? Many writers do fear sharing their work, but will your fear make you so timid that you wait years to start really writing, from your heart, putting on the page the experiences, feelings, and thoughts that make you unique? Finding your best material may require an audience. With a group of writers committed to helping you with your writing, you can discover your best subjects and better understand your work.

Writers are continually asking themselves questions about their own writing experience. Know which ones you want to answer at this stage in your career. Do you need help figuring out what to write, or do you start well and then get stuck in the middle of promising stories, poems, and essays and need help persevering? Do you want to share drafts of your work for feedback? Do you want to know where to submit your work for publication?

It isn't easy to determine what you need from a writing group, especially if you've never been in one before. Many writers join or start writing groups because they want to improve their writing skills. But learning to write isn't *solely* about getting technical advice. It also involves gaining knowledge about the writing process, about the sources of your creativity, about trust, commitment, and discipline.

Those of you who have taken many writing workshops or been through an MFA program may be already burdened by "instructional baggage." You may need to distance yourself both from criticisms and from the kind of praise you've received in those settings to get back to what's in your heart.

Two years after getting her undergraduate degree in English, Jacqueline decided to return to school for a creative writing degree. At the time, she wanted to "go through the fire" of rigorous criticism and education about writing. She wanted to meet high standards, to be compelled to write and rewrite her work until it was as excellent as it could be. More nurturing programs were not options because she felt they would not bring her to the height of her potential.

This view is reasonable and common enough to many writers. But Jacqueline neglected to ask herself how a different environment would encourage her creativity. What did she learn—and what *didn't* she learn—when pushed? Had she ever been nurtured as a writer, and did she know what *that* would do to her work? There were other important questions: Did she need to sharpen her technical and critical skills, or did she need to find the sources for her richest material? If she needed to do both, which should she work on first?

After finishing her MFA degree at a competitive program, during which time she wrote proficiently but sometimes without passion, she joined our writing group. During one meeting, while listening to herself spell out what was and wasn't working in her story draft, an insight came to her: "This environment, with both support and critical feedback from the others, is helping me! This is exactly what I need now." Jacqueline realized she required something else along with the high standards to grow as a writer.

It is that something else, that contribution to your writing you cannot find on your own, that you can get from a writing group. Most writing groups, like writing workshops, focus on *product*. However, your writing group can also address the writing *process*: that is, you can assist one another at all stages of writing, so that even if you don't have a finished story to be critiqued, you can discover new approaches to generating ideas for stories, open up and develop your range of topics for writing, experiment with different writing styles and voices, hone your writing skills, and explore new venues for sharing your work with others.

Figuring out what you are looking for in a writing

group *before* your first meeting will make your experience more rewarding.

Finding Other Group Members

If you think you want to belong to a writing group, how do you find other writers to work with?

It's impossible—we promise you—*not* to find writing partners. We know because at different times all of us have sought and found like-minded writers through local newspapers, journals, colleges, libraries, community organizations—even the Internet. One of our members put up flyers on telephone poles all over Harvard Square inviting others to join a writing group in Cambridge, Massachusetts. As she was working, a policeman approached and informed her that it was illegal to put flyers on telephone poles and it was his job to remove the flyers every few days. He spared her a citation but took a flyer for himself because he'd been considering joining a writing group.

In researching writing groups, we learned that quite a few start as a way to continue meeting with members of a workshop or class that is ending. After working together for eight or more weeks, members know one another's writing and how each gives and receives feedback on working drafts. This familiarity can only help as they form a writing group.

If you're new to town or to writing and unsure of how to locate other writers, you can enroll in a class at a local library, university, community college, or continuing education program. You can also find potential group members by placing an ad in the newspaper or a flyer on a bulletin board in a library, bookstore, coffee shop, or other writers' hangouts. If you choose to advertise for new members, don't pack too much into your ad. Include the essentials and your telephone number and then talk in depth with potential members.

Another way to gather members is to reach out to writers you already know who you think would benefit from a writing group. Choose individuals whose personalities and work you respect. If you don't get along with them, if they're not as serious about writing as you are, or if they're interested in writing Harlequin romances while you're writing literary short stories, then you'll probably learn the hard way that you're incompatible. If, instead, you know other writers, but not particularly well or personally, be bold enough to approach them with your idea of forming a group. Meet for coffee and talk about the kind of group you want to create. Like you, they may crave the company of other writers and an audience for their work.

Some writers (usually experienced ones) tell us they would *never* join a group with writers they didn't already know well. As one writer said, "Think of all the time and energy you're going to spend with these people." She wants the "right" people for her group. But how do you know who is "right" in advance?

The "Right" People for Your Group

When forming a writing group, your main priority is to bring together enthusiastic writers willing to explore the "outer bounds" of what you can do together. Ideally, group members are committed to a process of identifying individual needs and structuring a group around those needs. To find out whether potential group members are interested in the kind of work you wish to do, you will need to be direct in your initial discussions with them. Ask them if they have the time for a writing group and if they're serious about helping one another. Talk to them about their writing and exchange work. Don't consider the exchange an "application" to the writing group. You are reading one another's work to determine whether group members will have anything constructive to say about the writing. As one writer told us, "You have to respect the artistic goals, if not the quality, of the other writers' work." If writers say they'll know better whether they want to join after they meet the other group members, allow them to come to a few meetings on a trial basis. Understand that writers, especially those who have been in groups that didn't serve their needs, will want to avoid joining a group that isn't right for them.

Writers often work with others who have similar writing experience and who write in the same genre or genres—poetry, fiction, nonfiction, playwriting, or screenwriting. However, sticking to one genre may undermine the melding of dissimilar perspectives that is a source of the group's synergy. If you're an experienced writer finding yourself blocked, a beginner's enthusiasm for writing can be a great jump start for your work. In addition, each member needn't be a fiction writer: the most insightful readers may be those working in other genres. Being unschooled in the "rules" of a genre, their eyes and ears are fresh.

In sum, try to find writers who share your most basic creative needs and who can expose you to new approaches to writing. Potential group members will need to discuss two sets of issues: artistic concerns, such as the type of writing your group members do and the ways you will work together, and organizational concerns, including when, where, and for how long you will meet, and how to make group meetings run smoothly.

Artistic Considerations

To work effectively in the beginning stages of a writing group, members must take into account their artistic commonalities and differences, as well as their strengths and weaknesses as writers and group participants. Before you consider scheduling meetings, compare your artistic goals with those of potential group members. As you look for members (or consider joining an existing group), do not decide in advance that differences are necessarily problems. Ask yourself what you can gain from the process of building a working relationship *together*.

Differences in Experience and Commitment

When forming or joining a group, look first at each individual's writing experience and commitment. A writer just beginning to write, even a talented one, will probably not know enough about writing to give the kind of in-depth, sophisticated feedback a seasoned writer with extensive workshop experience can provide. Experienced writers have told us that belonging to a group with too many beginners would be difficult for them, particularly if the group critiques members' drafts. "You're reading and writing comments on pages of stuff that's not very good, slaving over it," said one writer, "doing more work than the writer did. I start to wonder why I'm doing it at all." Beginning writers may also be less productive, making the group less fulfilling for more ad-

42

vanced writers. However, one writer pointed out that if the group acknowledges the differences between advanced and beginning writers, a unique exchange can occur. Advanced writers can teach beginners, training them, in effect, to become better group participants. Indeed, new writers often bring a great deal of enthusiasm and novelty to writing groups, and if they are eager to learn from those with more experience, a mixed group will flourish.

Even if all of you are beginners, you can learn much from one another to improve your writing. Most important, we believe, members should possess a strong commitment to writing, no matter what their level of experience. You want writers in your group who are serious about their writing and who will be active, enthusiastic participants.

Genre Differences

Most of our group members define themselves as fiction writers. However, half of us also write and have published poetry, memoir, and nonfiction. When freewriting together from a prompt, we write in different genres and often encourage each other to experiment. Listening to both poetry and prose written from the same prompt suggests new approaches to our material. As fiction writers, we marvel at how poetic inventions turn on language and personal associations, and we try using the prompts as starting points for free associations that lead to stories. Those of us who tend to write from personal experience dare to explore the imaginative leaps made in fiction. Our writing horizons are broadened by genre differences in our freewriting.

Occasionally, someone will bring poems for feedback from the group. We respond to each poem by discussing what sounds natural, what does and does not seem solidly written, and what lacks interest. Those who write poetry speak most often, and the others learn by listening to them. Other fiction writers in mixed-genre groups tell us that they came to understand poetry better by having poets in their writing groups.

In an all-poets writing group Jacqueline joined two years ago, she wrote prose poems and short-short stories that emphasized language. Being in the group made her extremely conscious of language in a way she'd never been in a fiction-writing group or in fiction workshops in her MFA program.

"It was an interesting time for me, paying more attention to how I captured small details instead of how I structured a story or captured a facet of a character's personality," she says. When that group formally critiqued members' poetry, Jacqueline gave her gut reactions to the poems. "Discussing poetry challenged me. It wasn't always comfortable, but I learned a great deal about reading poems."

Expect, however, to receive less technical, more subjective feedback on your writing from those unfamiliar with your preferred genre than from those with experience. Novices can be refreshing in their candor, but if you want thorough, specific feedback on poetry, you should join or form a group with a significant number of poets—and likewise with personal essay writers, nonfiction writers, and journalists. (Many fiction writers can switch from short stories to novels without any trouble.) The point is to work with people who can speak intelligently and in depth about your genre.

Working with Common Interests

Your writing group ought to be a place where you learn about new possibilities for your work. Therefore, as you decide what your group will do during its meetings, consider ways to respond creatively to the full range of artistic interests and needs represented by members. A combination of activities can enrich all the writers in your group.

If most of your members are beginning writers, for example, each can keep a "process journal" while writing at home. In a process journal, you record instances when you sat down to write, what inspired you, how it felt to write, and how you assessed the writing you did. Then, at meetings, members can read from these journals and discuss one another's insights. These conversations can be most helpful for beginning writers.

Whether you're beginners or advanced writers, you can also read published work together and discuss it in the group. Our group has often talked about (but not yet tried) having each member bring in copies of a published piece she wishes she had written. Such an exercise benefits not only the writer sharing the selection but the others, who learn what she is striving for.

Playwrights and screenwriters, dealing almost entirely in dialogue, can ask a group to help them dramatize their work. In Tucson, screenwriting groups exist in which members not only critique each other's screenplays but read them aloud, with members taking on the characters' roles. For screenwriting, as well as playwriting, it is particularly helpful to hear one's lines read aloud by others, and this special need, inherent in the genre, can certainly be met by a writing group.

Responding to common artistic interests among group members is a continual challenge that requires ingenuity and a willingness to experiment.

Organizational Details

Just as all writers pick up the pen (or sit at the computer) at different times and deal uniquely with the writing process, every writing group is distinct. However, the issues described below arise frequently during start-ups.

How Many Members?

Many writing groups thrive with four or five committed members. You can start with this number, and in time you may grow. Decide, though, in the first few meetings what will be your group's upper limit. If you opt for as many as ten, as we once did, you will need to allot at least two and a half hours for meetings. To do one free-writing exercise together with ten people, including reading and commenting, will take you an hour and a half: twenty–thirty minutes of writing and about an hour for readings and discussion. To leave time for critiquing drafts of members' work, you will have to hold nearly three-hour meetings.

Groups with as many as ten members often include some who are erratic in their attendance. A core group of five or six can assure continuity between meetings, allowing the other members to come and go at will. After meeting for three years, we have a core group of six who attend regularly and are the source of new ideas for group activities. The others, for various reasons, come less often but are welcome.

Adding Members

When consecutive meetings included fewer than six, our group members sometimes suggested new writers for the group—acquaintances or friends who wanted to join. Some of these writers remained with us, others moved on. Particularly during our second year, we decided to keep our group small. We were writing and reading productively, and one member was bringing sections of her novella for us to read at successive meetings. It wasn't, it seemed, a good time to add a new person. We were not closed to new members in the future, but at that time we were satisfied with our group's size. Particularly if the group has gained momentum—working well together, understanding in depth one another's writing and writing process—it may not be the time to add new members. (See pages 167–71 for more on new members.)

Writing groups may need to discuss and then vote on whether to expand, as well as decide whether to accept particular writers. It helps to explain your group's purpose and structure to a prospective member *before* her first meeting, and to be as candid as possible if a new member isn't working out. However, we have found that allowing each person to decide for herself whether she belongs in our group helps all of us take responsibility for our individual writing efforts. Even if you're an aggressive person who likes to be in control, you don't want to be policing your writing group.

Gender
Over time we have conducted workshops at the University of Arizona's Extended University for Tucson writers looking to create their own writing groups. We never thought gender was an important issue in forming a group, but both male and female members of these workshops asked us about it. We explained that although we have no male members in our group, this is mainly because the women who started it were friends, not because

they or any of the subsequent members prefer working exclusively with women.

In discussions with our workshop participants and members of other writing groups, we find that gender differences do not adversely affect the artistic focus of writing groups. On the contrary, members tell us they appreciate hearing how the opposite sex feels about their writing. Especially if a member is writing about gender-sensitive topics—for example, if a female has written a story about a troubled marriage from the point of view of both wife and husband—a male reader's feedback about the story may help the writer avoid stereotyping.

On the other hand, we have talked to women who prefer working in women-only writing groups because of the subject matter of their work. A woman writer may not feel comfortable sharing her story about sexual abuse with men, for example. However, most writers we have encountered, including the members of our own group, believe gender is only one of many factors that shape a group's dynamic.

Where to Meet

Writing groups usually meet in a quiet place where members can sit comfortably, hear one another speak, and concentrate. A logical choice is at a member's home, either in the same house every time or at different members' homes. Our group rotates the role of host so that everyone occasionally has the luxury of not needing to travel to a meeting. The host provides food and beverages, but a few group members always bring additional snacks. At the end of each meeting, we decide where to meet next. One problem with this arrangement is that members who miss a meeting need to call around, or be called, to find out where the next meeting will be. To avoid this problem, you can set up a schedule in advance or meet at the same person's house each time, provided that's not a burden.

Some writing groups have access to meeting rooms in libraries, schools, or other buildings. Other groups meet at restaurants or cafes. The only difficulty with this last option is that eating establishments are rarely quiet enough, especially for group members who write together or read work aloud. Some people are easily distracted by others walking by or chatting at the next table. Using an empty corner of a restaurant or cafe may help members stay focused.

When to Meet and for How Long

Many fledgling writing groups spend most of their first meeting going from person to person trying to figure out what day or night members can meet. Particularly in a large group, finding a common meeting time can be difficult. Our group happened upon Friday night as the only time all of us were free, and we've stuck with it, although many of us are weary by the end of the week. Some writers say they would prefer to meet in the mornings, when their minds are most clear. Certainly, if you have gathered together writers with free daytime hours, meeting then will avoid the exhaustion that often besets nighttime groups.

From our own and other writers' experience, we've found that in the beginning, you should meet together at least twice a month. Any less than that and you don't get to know each other quickly enough. Groups that meet once a month can break down rapidly because few feel invested, committed, or intrigued by their group.

It is preferable to set up a schedule for meeting times and places in advance rather than planning meeting by meeting. Members can mark off the writing group meetings in their calendars and avoid conflicts, and the group doesn't have to spend time at the end of each meeting discussing these details.

Our meetings last about two hours. That gives us time for writing, discussion, and either critiquing a volunteer's writing or doing other work together. We ask that everyone arrive on time. However, as we became better friends over time, and because some wonderful cheeses, fruits, and breads were often laid out on the table when we arrived, some meetings started late. Now we arrive a little early or stay after the meeting to socialize. It's not that we don't want to socialize. We simply feel the time we are willing to give to our writing cannot be compromised.

Leadership

Some writing groups have a designated leader, usually someone with greater writing experience than the others or with particular skill at helping groups do their work. Leaders generally organize meetings and conduct discussions. In some cases they teach the group as needed about the basics of writing and assign readings for group discussion, thus moving things along during and between meetings. The leader may or may not consider herself part of the group. In some cases, the leader is paid, particularly if teaching is one of her responsibilities. These paid leaders usually make decisions for the group, such as selecting the sequence and frequency of the group's activities (critiquing, reading published writing, and so forth).

Usually, it is easier to get a group started with someone in charge. Leaders are particularly helpful to members who have never been in a writing group before or to quiet, shy members who will be relieved that someone else has taken responsibility for arranging schedules and deciding how to run the group. Even experienced group members will appreciate the efficiency a leader often brings to the start-up. If the leader is also a teacher, there is an added benefit.

On the other hand, many members prefer to share responsibility for organizing and running the group. Our group has never had or needed a leader because members do the leadership work themselves: Susan R. told us about a writing exercise based on illustrations that she did with her students and suggested we try it in a meeting. Beth brought in some beautiful handmade books she'd created in a class, and we elaborated on her work in a writing exercise. Dawn brought up our group's low attendance one night, engaging us in a difficult, but ultimately helpful, discussion. The advantage of not having a formal leader is that you can work together in a democratic, consensual way—so long as things move along. The disadvantage is that it can be hard to get anything decided, never mind accomplished, with a group of people unwilling to take either individual or collective responsibility for the group.

Annie, a Tucson poet and member of one of our writing group workshops, believes all groups should have leaders. She feels strongly about this because her experience in a group that lacked a leader was discouraging. Members were reluctant to share their work and to suggest new activities. Instead, they expected the host, in whose home the meetings were always held, to lead. But the host did so grudgingly, and since she couldn't persuade the others to share leadership, she soon grew weary of the job. By default, the group became not only leaderless but directionless.

To share leadership in a group, Annie says—and we agree—it's important to have people in your group who will lead willingly, in a friendly, unaffected way that doesn't disempower quieter members. Keep in mind as you gather writing group members: will each take some responsibility for addressing the group and for laying out options for activities during meetings? If you are not comfortable leading, think about whether you can prod yourself a little for the sake of your writing. Consider this: much beginning writing lacks authority. The voice doesn't fly off the page, saying, "Here I am, and here is what I have to say!" Taking a small risk in a group—for example, by saying, "I'll read first" or "I will bring in a story next week"—may make you feel so good that you carry that energy straight into your writing.

Another approach is to rotate leadership. Each meeting, someone (the host if you're meeting at one another's homes) is responsible for keeping discussion moving and for checking with everyone when a group decision must be made. In this way, everyone gets a chance to lead and grow. In time, you may be able to abandon assigned leadership because the group has become fluid, interactive, and healthy on its own.

How to Structure Meetings

Preparing for the First Meeting: Being Open

Take an open mind into your first writing group meeting. On your way to the event, try not to be concerned about scheduling, personality differences, and how "good" you are as a writer. Instead, have faith in yourself and your commitment to writing—even if it falters and makes you weep at night.

On the drive or walk over, meditate on what you want for yourself, but don't focus on what you want to the exclusion of anything else. To get the most out of the first meeting, you will need to put aside your focus on yourself and your own writing long enough to concentrate on what the others say. Remember that you're in a group not only for the sake of your own writing, but to help others with their writing. Suppose some members want to write together and others do not. Perhaps your "group" could be divided into subgroups that occasionally meet on different nights. Such an idea might not occur to members set on a certain schedule or agenda before coming to the meeting.

Unfortunately, in many first meetings, a few individuals say what they want out of the group, some say nothing at all, and no one actually responds to each other's statements. To avoid this, consider that you need to "co-create" this group, to carefully communicate and listen to one another's needs. In this way you will discover how to organize and begin working together. Any group is weakest in the beginning because no one has invested enough yet and people have different needs. Someone wants to learn about craft and someone else wants to talk personally about fears of rejection. If the group is not open-minded, you would call that an impasse and give up.

Pay more attention to what you have in common and less to what you don't. Wait before deciding that differences are insurmountable. You have to be open to where the group will take you in the same way you are when you sit down to write a story. You write a line and follow it, moving on a new path. If you're too tight, you'll stop and remind yourself of what the story is "supposed" to be about. You'll say, "Wait a minute! I meant to be writing about Roger, a teenage boy obsessed with Richard Nixon. He's not supposed to be playing the clarinet in his underwear in front of his father's business friends." If you're open while generating your story line, you will pick up his melody and let him play his tune. For the moment, you'll forget about your plans and let the writer inside you take over. This way, and this way only—in writing and in writing groups—you will create something authentic and new.

Conducting the First Meeting

After you've settled into your seats at your first meeting, members ought to introduce themselves, including saying something about who they are and what kind of writing they do.

After introductions, we suggest you take a risky and exciting step. Instead of *talking* about the artistic and organizational considerations that will need to be discussed, try *writing* together about them first. Have group members clear their minds and imagine there are no limits. Imagine everyone in the room is committed to writing and eager to help and be helped. Imagine the ideal writing *community*—no matter how unrealistic you think it is. You could picture a group of writers who support and assist one another in their work, who are honest, insightful, and sensitive to other people's artistic and personal concerns. See yourself coming home from writing group meetings with poems and stories started, with ideas for revision, with a brand-new outlook on writing that gets you over your block.

In your first meeting, try the "Ideal Writing Group" exercise:

Getting Started

*Every person takes a sheet of paper. In a ten-minute
freewrite, describe your ideal writing group, writing as
quickly and as honestly as you can. Be specific—don't
wax poetic for too long about the good feelings in the
room. What happens at meetings? What do you walk
away with? What happens between meetings?*

When starting our writing group, we had to speak
clearly and honestly about our needs. We had to overcome shyness and fear, and we had to think big to *create*
a writing group that could help us. The next part of the
exercise encourages members to put their visions on the
table for the whole group to discuss:

*Members read their "Ideal Writing Group" freewrites
aloud, then discuss them, explaining how these descriptions relate to their individual needs as writers. Think
only about this moment: don't start hedging, saying, "I
know in a year, I'll need more help with revision." Talk
about what motivated you to write what you did* now.
*When everyone has finished, try to talk as a group about
the similarities and differences of these visions.*

This discussion of the ideal writing group will lead naturally to a conversation about most of the artistic and
practical details of your meetings, including when,
where, and how often to meet.

To structure the discussion, begin a two-part conversation about the group's organization and purpose—
about what we call "Core Group Issues." Half of your
discussion will take place during your first meeting, and
then, after a break of a week or two, you will join again
to continue talking and begin making decisions. Start at
your first meeting with this exercise:

Through discussion, identify issues about the writing group that matter most to participants—how to avoid destructive criticism, for example, whether to do writing exercises, the time of the meeting, the distance to the meeting place, and so forth. Everyone should take notes and keep track of areas of agreement and disagreement.

As you discuss these issues, clarify important values to the group, particularly artistic concerns: Perhaps genre differences worry a nonfiction writer in your group because she suspects her work won't be considered literary enough by the fiction writers. If she expresses such a fear, open up the discussion. Ask members to talk about how they feel about nonfiction. Look for "win-win" solutions. For example, a nonfiction writer could conduct a session about nonfiction. Or her work could be critiqued by only those writers who are interested in nonfiction.

In the first meeting, begin working out the details of your group's goals and structure. Be flexible and open to compromise.

Don't expect to decide everything during your first meeting, and as you talk, try not to dwell on *figuring out* how the group will work. You can't *make* trust, honesty, commitment, or synchronous schedules *happen* by discussing them. All you can do is create a likelihood that they will emerge. These issues will continue to matter throughout the life of your group. Let your "Core Group Issues" conversation end when you have thirty minutes left to your meeting.

For the final activity, do a short writing exercise that has nothing to do with how you'll structure your group, one that gives all of you a sense of what it's like to write together. Since many group members may be feeling anxious at the first meeting, you could try freewriting together on the word "challenges" or "fear" and then read these pieces aloud. (See chapter 4 for many examples of writing prompts.) You'll get to hear one another read—an important way to start understanding each other's writing.

The Second, Third, and Fourth Meetings

All meetings require some structure, but no more, in the beginning, than a loose sense of ordered activities. During your second meeting, you will want to finish your discussion about important issues for each member, planning, by the end of the meeting, a set of activities for the first two months of meetings. You may want to add to this exchange by doing the exercise "Defining Individual Needs."

> *Each member writes freely for ten minutes on the following question: "What do I need from this writing group to make it worth committing my time and energy?" Be specific, avoiding generic responses such as "improvement in my writing." Instead, provide details of your writing goals that you believe the writing group can address. Members then read their writing aloud and discuss what they do and do not have in common.*

Responding to one another's writing is traditionally what writing groups do. But our writing group does more than that. It gives us new ideas for writing, it supports us, and it stimulates us to try new approaches. Your writing group can feed your creative process . . . but only if the group dedicates time to learning about one another's writing from more than just drafts for critiquing.

In our workshops with writers who want to form

groups, we try to set them on a course of exploring *process* as well as *product* with some exercises to help members get to know each other's writing. The following are good icebreakers for early meetings, and doing them will tell you much about your own writing process.

(1) Exchanging Work for the First Time. In the first meetings, you will want to gain a sense of each other's writing. Although you may have decided that your group will regularly critique members' writing, we suggest, before critiquing, that you have each participant share some work with the group that you don't critique formally. Instead, use this exchange as a chance for each writer to tell the group about her writing aspirations and to reflect on her process.

> *Each member should bring no more than ten pages of recent writing to share, either a whole piece or an excerpt. If desired, writers can bring two different selections—one piece they think is successful, another piece with which they are struggling. Give the group until the next meeting to read all the material. At the following session, have members talk about their own work, telling the group what they think is and is not working in their selections. Members might also compare the selections to their writing in general. Group members can jump in with comments on an individual's selections when it feels natural to do so. They can tell the writer what they liked about the work and a little about what wasn't as successful. (The group may want to set a time limit for each person so that no one runs on and each person's writing gets discussed.) But all group members will want to keep in mind that this is not a formal critique. The purpose of the exercise is to read some of each member's writing and hear how members talk about writing.*

(2) Exploring the Writing Process. Some writers need guidance in talking about their writing process with a group. This exercise helps members think about new topics for group work.

> *Members finish each of the following sentences, writing as much as they need to answer the question, even a paragraph or two.*
> *(1) The time of day when I usually write is . . .*
> *(2) The time of day I most like to write is . . .*
> *(3) The first thing I do when I sit down to write is . . .*
> *(4) My first fifteen minutes of writing go as follows: . . .*
> *(5) When I write, I'm most afraid of/that . . .*
> *(6) My ideas for writing come from . . .*
> *(7) If you were to observe me writing after half an hour of work, you would see . . .*
>
> *After writing, members read their responses to each of these questions aloud, tackling one question at a time. They discuss whatever intrigues and surprises them, elaborating on their answers.*

Although members should avoid judging any one answer as right or wrong, this exercise showed our group that writers who can be patient with themselves, who sometimes pause and stare out the window while at their writing desks, are less likely to get frustrated and give up. Also, writers who work during their optimum time of day are more likely to be productive.

(3) Sharing Writing Models. In a third exercise that works especially well in new groups, members bring in a published piece that they would love to have written themselves. Copies can be distributed and read between meetings, or, if the pieces are short, a few members can read their selections aloud and spread the exercise out

over a few weeks. When discussing each piece, have the person who brought it in talk about the strengths and weaknesses of the writing and explain how she thinks her work compares to the published work. Other group members may comment on the piece as well.

This exercise can overwhelm inexperienced group members because it highlights differences in artistic taste. However, such differences are not to be feared; they promise dynamic group discussions. Instead of judging the writing admired by one another, listen carefully to each group member tell you *why* she likes the work. In this way, you get inside one another's writing mind.

Writing Together

Whether or not your group plans to write together, we recommend that you do so during your first few meetings. Throughout our early months, we always wrote together and had each member read her work aloud. We talked informally about our process and about what we did and did not like about the topic and our approach.

Writing together during group meetings is an effective starting point for any group. By exposing raw writing to your group members, you encourage creativity and risk-taking. Writing groups that achieve this level of trust and openness feed members' personal artistic growth.

At the same time, when you listen to each other read freewriting aloud, you may envy someone's writing or feel insecure about your own. All writers have these feelings, and it helps to accept the fact that hundreds of differences exist between writers' skills. Some writers shine in freewriting; others freewrite awkwardly but revise so well that what was inchoate becomes graceful and seamless. Writers who freewrite often are bound to be looser and more fluid in these exercises than those just starting.

Don't be put off by these differences. Writing together teaches by example. Your own writing will grow under the influence of the voices you hear month after month in your group.

Veteran members of our group admit they still suffer some anxiety when it's their turn to read. Accept that you will feel tense doing something that is difficult. Writing itself is difficult, but you keep doing it.

Finally, when you write together, don't be fooled into believing what you write will be brilliant. Think of nothing at all except that you're not going to stop writing until someone says, "Time" (twenty minutes for a beginning group, building to forty-five minutes for an advanced group). By being nonjudgmental, you will learn to use your writing group as a source of inspiration, not intimidation.

Response and Discussion

As we began to sense our members' writing strengths and weaknesses, we started commenting briefly on the exercises we did together and continue to do so today. Each of us finds something different to point out to the writer; each of us responds differently to the same words. Someone can feel an incipient novel in a short piece and can even pull it out like thread from a spool. Others notice the strengths of the writer's voice, characterizations, or scenes. Listening to members comment on each other's writing helps us see where we might want to go next in our own, or where we are already heading without quite realizing it.

After a writing exercise, our group often moves naturally into a discussion of some general writing issue that developed from the freewrite: how characters come to life in one paragraph by way of a few telling details or why certain characters in stories we've loved are so memorable. Someone says she can't begin writing about a new character until she's thought through at least half the character's life, and then someone else laughs and explains that she just dives in and lets her characters come to life on the page and tell *her* what to write. More personal issues enter our discussions: how we struggle at home, for example, wondering whether we are revising too soon, ruining what's energetic and good in rough drafts. Sometimes group members ask pointed questions of other members: Are you avoiding writing the stories you need to write because you think they're ugly or frightening? How much do you care about this subject? Why did you choose to write about this character? Other times we talk about technical matters.

You will want to leave time for exchanges like these, which is why it is best not to pack your schedule with too many planned activities. Through talk, we have helped one another move past writing blocks, sometimes even solved writing problems on the spot. Someone says, "I can't believe how this author just jumps around from one character's mind to another's. Why can't I do that?" Well, *why not?* By talking to someone who uses a technique that is not as easy for you, you can learn about her process—and yours. You can also experiment with unfamiliar techniques during freewrites.

Critiquing Drafts

Because the business of critiquing is sometimes sensitive and always challenging, it may be helpful for groups to agree on guidelines before beginning. You can always change the rules when the group feels it appropriate. You need to decide whether you will schedule critiques of each member's work in advance or wait for volunteers.

Getting Started

Most writers coming into a group want deadlines, so assigning due dates early works well. You must discuss, as well, whether your group is willing to read works-in-progress, what kinds of feedback to give, how to structure the session so that everyone who wants to comment gets a chance, and whether to give written comments on drafts distributed in advance. Particularly if group members have participated in workshops in the past, they will have strong opinions on these issues. (See pages 126–31 for a detailed discussion about the range of approaches to critiquing, and for strategies and guidelines.)

One of the hardest things about getting a writing group started is that the most lasting benefits of working together come slowly. You have planned your group carefully. You possess a clear sense of what you and the others want out of the group, but so far no real insights into your own or one another's writing have occurred. You may not even have perfect attendance in the early stages. However, slow, uneven beginnings are natural. Members are not yet invested in the writing group. With time, as you begin to see the benefits of your meetings, you will sense a core commitment and purpose to your group.

Be patient. You are assembling a group of people to aid one another with their writing—something they care a great deal about. Your members may have many years of experience writing without this kind of assistance, and for some, the setting will be so new and unfamiliar they will put up obstacles. Do not fear conflict; just lay a good foundation. No matter what type of group you create, vision, flexibility, and openness will be what hold it together.

Our first meeting had an edge to it, a dangerous sensation of risk that you will come to appreciate in your group and in your own writing. The decision to cover new ground and try new approaches together inspired enough enthusiasm, excitement, and fear to make us active participants from the start. This was no dull planning meeting: we had work to do!

4   Writing Prompts

> When we do not trouble ourselves about whether or not
> something is a work of art, if we just act in each moment
> with composure and mindfulness, each moment of our
> life is a work of art.
>
> —Thich Nhat Hanh
> *Peace Is Every Step: The Path of*
> *Mindfulness in Everyday Life*

We ordinarily refer to "exercise" as the thing we do when we practice a skill. We exercise the arm to make the stroke, the fingers to play the scale, the vocal cords to warm up. We use exercises—repetitions of technical elements—to own our game and improve. Yet the repetitious act may feel or, worse yet, may become mindless. As W. Timothy Gallwey suggests in *The Inner Game of Tennis*, we should practice a skill attentively, by paying attention to what we do as we learn to do it better. All good athletes and performers know there is nothing mindless about practice.

Most people don't think of their writing as exercise unless they recall grammar drills from grade school. But every time writers sit down to write, it *is* a form of practice. First, the courageous act of taking that seat at your desk and writing day after day, no matter what gets on the page, is a kind of practice. Next, paying attention to what happens as you write—sweaty hands or sudden excitement—letting it guide and teach you, is a way of practicing your craft. For example, when Dawn writes from the four elements, she is always surprised by the connection between the unpremeditated prompt and the stories from her own life she wants to write about. Her success in writing from this prompt in the group encouraged her to write more spontaneously at home and helped her get at her stories with less effort. We have learned in our group to commit to the process of writing rather than focusing on product. We use prompts to work together mindfully, in fast, unedited writing, and to learn from what we do.

Part of what we've learned is to change our writing prompts to meet our changing needs as writers. From one word to several words, to sentences, to elements picked from envelopes, to plastic sandwich bags filled with small objects, our prompts help us arrive at the connection in our writing to the stories of our lives.

The prompts in the first section, "Working with Words," appear in the order we used them from our first meeting to present time. The other prompts are grouped by category, not chronology. Use the prompts in any order you like. To begin with one word may seem easier than using four elements, but truly, each prompt will engage each writer differently; there isn't one best way to order them. As we came to develop the exercises for our specific needs, they progressed in intensity and then began to serve as links to larger issues of story, such as plot and character. We also gradually increased our writing time together from twenty or thirty minutes to forty-five to sixty minutes. This time factor increased the level of complexity in the prompts. We suggest that you read through all the prompts and simply choose one to start with. Remember to focus on the group's needs when choosing prompts.

In this chapter, we also include excerpts of the writing we did in response to the prompts. The excerpts appear as they were written with only spelling corrections. You read exactly what we heard when we first read our work aloud in the group.

Search for new prompts. Steal ideas like you steal glimpses into the lives of the people around you. Writers take the world's offerings and make something new from what they observe, know, and feel. Use our prompts and gather your own. Change those offered here to fit your needs. Experiment: give yourself up to this process, and don't stop writing!

In writing from prompts, some of us began in the real stories of our lives and moved into fiction or poetry during the writing. Others leapt into an imaginative place immediately. Where we go in the writing does not matter much, but paying attention to what the journey can teach us does. Use these prompts in and out of your writing group, and soon you will know what you need to do next in your craft. Your writing will show you. That is the practice of writing, the profession's work.

Working with Words

When we start something new, it is comforting to begin with a tiny step. We test the waters, and although we put our big toe in that freezing, rushing stream to decide whether to cross, our toe still gets wet. No matter how small our beginning, we are still in the stream.

Words
In our group, we began writing from one word. However, one word, like one toe in the stream, can lead to surprising places. Don't think that because you start

small it is *easier*. In our group, we started with the words *fathers, China, home,* and *hair*. These turned out to be loaded words, taking us into places we knew and usually avoided, places we often feared, places we'd already lived in far too long. We got plenty wet and realized we'd been planning to go in all along, no matter the temperature or speed of the water.

To begin, we thought we'd have one person bring a word to each meeting, but then, for that one person, the writing was less spontaneous. We decided instead to choose a word together at meetings. There are many ways to find a word. Look through the books on your host's shelf or in your own journal and use the first word that strikes you. Have group members write out several words on slips of paper and put them into an envelope. Carry the envelope from meeting to meeting. However you find your words, let them be spontaneous for everyone in the group.

Even though we write from the same word, we are in separate worlds, as the following excerpts show. From the word *China*, Susan N. wrote,

China. I've never liked the word China, the idea of China, the large land mass, people mass, although I've always liked well enough the delicate china teacups of my mother's house, the translucent creamy sides, shapely and strong, tea steaming off the top, thin and curved against the lips, the promise of conversation and cookies, at one time cigarettes, the privilege of women in the afternoon, taking pleasure in privilege, as at Wellesley in the late '60's, tea Wednesday and Friday afternoons served by the housemother—the cup, please, and do you take water, lemon, milk—and cookies, always the promise of lemon bars, sandies, sprawled along the soft sofas of the dormitory, women in all shapes, sizes, intellects, always with the regulation dress on Wednesday—jeans were okay on Friday—tea and privilege and pleasure. I went to tea to smoke. It was not a happy time, not because of the ritual, protocol, the air thick with women all doing the right thing, but because I was lost among the crumbs. . . .

From the same word, Jacqueline began,

China is the riptide swelling of all the places you have ever wanted to go. A game board sits in the corner, with small glass stones, all the size of fingernails, of young boys' thumbnails, and they are green, blue, yellow, and red. She pulls the board out of its niche and puts it in between her legs and points to a chair where I sit slowly and stare at the incense burning a gray trail toward the window.

China is her name, and her favorite pastime is to play board games with strangers, and she likes to intersperse the game with bits of her personal history. Like she was born in Cheyenne, Wyoming. Like she smoked marijuana when she was ten years old with her brother Billy. Like she had both her feet crunched under the tire of a dump truck when she was two, which, she says, is why her toes are so small, why the nails are little flecks of cartilage. . . .

When you hear the single-word prompt, start writing whatever images or thoughts come to mind in response to it. This writing may seem undirected, as if you were scrambling around. Notice in Susan N.'s excerpt, she does just that: she begins with initial images of the place, China, and then settles into teatime at Wellesley. Jacqueline moves right into a story and sketches out her main character, China. Freewriting has no rules; to "scramble around" is an excellent way to get started writing. If your hand is moving across the page, something eventually will take over and fall into focus.

Consider, too, that the words you choose may influence the kind of writing you do. Look at the following excerpts written from the word *home*, for example. Notice how, for both writers, childhood memories became the focus. Jo Anne wrote:

> I think of my childhood right away, the house I lived in for eighteen years, the town I stayed in for twenty-eight. I think of a place first, not feelings. Three rooms. Linoleum floors. A big black oil burner in the bedroom we all shared until I was almost four years old and my dad added two rooms to the house we were still renting. I think of the oven being turned on and the door kept open on cold winter mornings so we could be warm at the other end of the house, too. I think of the lines strung across the kitchen every Monday during the winter months so the clothes my mom had washed that day could dry—the ones that didn't fit on the large folding rack that she set up next to the oil burner. . . .

Susan R. wrote:

> Along with body, one of our most basic concepts. What is home for one person is never home for another—even in a house shared by many people. Home is a place in the brain, behind the eyes,

deep in the head. It's what you see when you close
your eyes.

I first felt at home in closets. A deep cedar
closet in the house I grew up in, slanting into a V
like a wedge of cheese. It was warm, it was dark,
it was a place where no one could find me. Where
I looked up at winter coats and imagined the people who belonged in them. . . .

A word like *home* is bound to take you back to the
walls of your own, as it did for Jo Anne and Susan R.,
even though their approaches to the word differ. Notice
how often you choose words that suggest deep connections to your life, and then note how you respond to
them. Do you always write from your past experiences?
Notice if other words suggest a strong link to childhood
memories. How do you respond to them? If you see patterns in your responses, change the kinds of words you
are choosing. Challenge yourself.

Our list of words grew to include *breathing, travelling,
childhood, desire, atmosphere, ghosts, appetite, maps, streets,
hair, dreaming/dreams,* and *shrines.*

Sentences

We played with words for several months, then
moved on to sentences. It was a logical, natural progression. Once we'd had our coffee and food, someone
would reach for a book from the host's shelf and start
browsing pages like aisles in a department store. We
found a line and dove in.

The following excerpts began with this line from Dorothy Allison's *Bastard Out of Carolina*: "Things come
apart so easily when they have been held together by
lies."

For some reason, when I think of that time in my life, I remember roses on the sofa, cabbages unfurling on the floor. Linoleum from the 40's or 50's, curling up, cracked. The upstairs hallway was dark and, in the hall, there was a window, an old lace tablecloth for a curtain. The room just at the head of the stairs had a big old four post bed, dark wood. That's where his grandmother died.

I remember rain, I remember dim light, the bare bulb in the lamp, walking into the room while he was sleeping. I liked to crawl into bed with him in the early morning. He was vulnerable, then, or maybe just quiet—anyway, at that moment, I'd think, what does it *matter* if he lies? What are lies anyway? They seemed so ephemeral. In the air, you know. Invisible. . . .

Beth

"Things come apart so easily when they have been held together by lies." But it takes time. It took minutes, at first, stretching out a response, waiting to see if it would hold, like how college was going, whom she was dating. Minutes to catch her mother's eye, hold the stare, dare her to protest, disagree, question. It was all a patina between them, an agreement. I will lie if you will believe, and it worked. But pins slowly dropped in the silences between them. . . .

Susan N.

"Things come apart so easily when they have been held together by lies." Bodies, cars, families. Life was an endless series of trips to repair places: hospitals, gas stations, family counselors. But the only things that held together, in the end, were those things that had strength in them to begin with. 1968 automobiles and the bodies of happy, healthy well-balanced people and families who prayed together and stayed together.

She couldn't have imagined that he could have come apart so easily, and yet every time she came home a different piece of him was gone. . . .

Susan R.

I can't write from this statement because its opposite seems truer. No. For some people, things held together with lies endure a lifetime exactly because they've been held together with lies, and to admit the truth, even a bit of it, would be to risk all the comfort and stability a lifetime of lies can get you. I think of marriages—not all but many—if not exactly held together with lies, then with half truths and the habit of suppressing. . . .

Jo Anne

For Jo Anne, the prompt led her to think about her parents' marriage and the institution of marriage. For the other three writers, the prompt led them to short fictions about emergencies and lies, making the original sentence imply many things at once.

It's interesting to consider what impact the original writer's voice may have on what you write. In this case, most of us had read Dorothy Allison's novel, and our freewriting reflected the mood she'd created. If you know a work well, it might be a good source for prompts.

You could choose to emulate a particular writer's style as a way of experimenting with your own writing. On the other hand, it might be limiting because you may get "stuck in the book," thinking or hearing the voice of the original writer.

There is a big difference between writing from one word and from an entire sentence. As you try these two prompts, notice how your group responds to each. In our group, the sentences elicited different responses: some found it easier to write from a sentence because it suggested a story; others found a sentence too limiting. What kind of freedom or limitation do you experience with each prompt? Experiment. Try using a word one meeting and a sentence the next and observe what happens.

Impromptu Prompts

When one word isn't enough, and a sentence is too much, we often use "impromptu prompts," or what Beth refers to as a "premise" for writing. These situations encapsulate so much in their suggestiveness that many of us have had good writing experiences with them.

Our impromptu prompts include *Describe a time when you've enjoyed eating food*, *Sunday mornings*, and *Fear of forgetting the names of colors*. When we wrote from one line—*I kissed a _____ once*—Daphne created a poem. She says she had no idea what she was going to write about when she first heard the prompt:

I did not consciously think at all when I was writing that piece that ended up being a poem. I just took the prompt and took the first image and line

that came to me. I didn't make any conscious decisions about form, language, images.

The poem begins:

I kissed a midwife while my friend lay spread eagle,
   belly rising.
I kissed an athlete. His scent of sweat under dark blank pits
   made me want to cry.
I kissed a student. In the hallway, on the sly, on the cheek,
   guessing.
I kissed my mother full on her soft slender lips.
   Her mouth was crooked from a root canal, her face
   crumpled. She was silly, soft, weak, old.
I kissed my teacher. He touched my young breasts under
   my tight light blue sweater.
   "I just couldn't help myself," he said.
I kissed my grandmother, her cheek sunken; I felt the bone
   of her jaw,
   tasted the brown mottled spots on her skin.
I have kissed, touched, and held.
I have not kissed. . . .

Daphne's first line simply popped into her head,
and then she was in it and writing. She says,

I never did kiss a midwife. None of these images
are real. I don't even know where they came from.
To me, they were part of the moment when we
started writing. The people, the professional and
personal relationships that were present. It all
came out of that experience.

Writing Together

When Daphne read, we all sat listening, held there by her images, all of which had emerged spontaneously. We had giggled at the cuteness of this prompt when someone first suggested it, but for Daphne, it became a doorway. As she says, some of her best writing occurs when she doesn't know what she is going to write about. We can't know what is going to happen every time we sit down to write.

For instance, one night we wrote from this impromptu prompt: *A beautiful woman gets her hand cut off with a chain saw.* Beth suggested it and we all groaned and laughed at the absurdity of it. Or perhaps it was the macabre beneath it? But when we read aloud we were amazed to hear similar themes, situations, and images arising from our writings. We wrote about our bodies, images of ourselves, the mutilation of flesh and spirit. We wrote about our sisters and mothers, about being women. Look at the similarities in these two excerpts:

I.

I thought of the rapid way the needle shoots dye beneath the skin and of the Sioux women how they used to cut a finger off in grief, of Japanese women cutting their thick dark hair. Ritual violence. The body as sacrifice, the body as sacrament, the body as metaphor. For *what*—

A beautiful woman stands beneath a willow tree, she must be young, yes, and slender, her hair must be long, the longer her hair, the more we are afraid for her, afraid for whatever shadow falls from the sky, afraid of the man, this is what we know will happen—even if the music doesn't rise, even if the sky doesn't darken. I couldn't sleep, what with mutilation of the body always on my mind. . . .

Well. This is what happens when you watch too much TV. I stood in front of the mirror and said this rather sternly: the city is not dangerous. Night hides nothing. I put on my boots and my jacket and I started going out on walks. The little mother voice told me: you must do what you fear.

II.

And she stands before grandfather's mirror. I think, she's free now. She's free. She's watching her freedom return to her and she stands perfectly still for the first time in years. I brush her hair, stroke it gently as she watches her body fill itself up. He died, and she's emancipated, and I'm sad because her freedom was given to her, not unwanted, but unsought. She's holding her wrist—gently at first—then she rubs it harder and harder, and the skin gets red fast. She's crying. She's holding her wrist across her bloated belly and freedom is hard to come by. It's a chain reaction—and she cries out, He might as well have cut off my hand!

Like an escaped slave, like a prisoner, a traitor, she loses a limb, a part of herself for ever thinking of leaving him.

No, I whisper back, you are a beautiful woman.

The prompt had been spontaneous, yet through our writing we were connected. This happens often: we share gestures, language, images, a kind of collaboration of our writing minds.

Impromptu prompts are challenging. Create this kind of prompt at the meeting just before you write, or fill an envelope with impromptu prompts and choose one at each meeting.

The Four Elements—Stories in a Shoe Box

Our group, having been together for a while, has a kind of organic rhythm: we can sense when we are using a prompt that is working for us all and when it is time to move on to something different. One exercise that held us in its grip for several months we came to call "the four elements."

One evening we talked about how we start stories, how we get our initial ideas. Dawn described one author's "trick" for starting stories. The writer kept a shoe box filled with slips of papers in his closet. He wrote down his observations of people, places, objects, and situations and put them in the box. Then, when he went to write, he'd pull out a few slips of paper and begin a story from them.

We decided we could do this, too. We made envelopes that night and labeled them Situation, Place, Object, and Character. Then each of us wrote several of each element on slips of paper and filled the envelopes. Each time we met thereafter, we pulled one element from each envelope and wrote for forty-five minutes. We passed the envelopes from house to house, and when we'd emptied those envelopes, we made more, writing from this prompt for the rest of that year.

The success of this prompt was due to many things: at the time we stumbled onto it, we were coming together as a cohesive and supportive group. We were comfortable with writing and reading together and taking more risks. For all of us, this prompt asked us to push past our individual comfort zones. Some of us used the prompt to write memoir only. Some of us wrote fiction. Dawn says,

> With the elements, we had the outline of a story not yet written, and all I had to do was begin and let my own experiences fill it out, let each element of the prompt guide the shape of the piece as I moved toward something I didn't know I'd write before we began.

One night we wrote from the following elements: *lost wallet, botanical gardens, an old hat,* and *Scorpion Man.* Scorpion Man was a character Dawn had put in the envelope months before. In fact, she'd forgotten all about him. She began the freewrite in her own voice, almost like a journal. Then, as she continued to write, she fell into a story about this character. She kept two narrative voices going at once, one telling the story, one commenting on it at the same time, almost as if she were conversing with the story as she wrote it. Note how the rest of the elements appear in these excerpts from her freewriting:

> He would be an eight-year-old boy with soft petals of red for hair clinging to a much too large and round and perfect forehead. And he'd almost be translucent, his skin so pale that around his temples you could see the one large blue vein pulsing deliberately under it. He'd call himself Scorpion Man.
>
> Mona would start it. She'd be the baby-sitter who arrived every day after three to watch him when his mother went to work the night shift. Mona would be tall and thin from head to toe, with long black stringy hair dyed in purples or

reds, depending, which she'd usually cover with an old gray felt hat. She'd wear red and white striped stockings and too big combat boots, a black see-through dress and only her bra and underwear underneath. A wiry, slippery modern day Olive Oyle. And he'd not love her, but be fascinated by her. . . .

I want the mom—I don't know her name—to be completely unable to reach Scorpion Man, like the night when she comes home from work and wakes him up to say goodnight, and she launches into a parade of descriptions. All the crazy and not so exciting customers she's waited on tonight. She gets stuck on one and just keeps describing this fat little man with gray hair sprouting out (like a poodle!) right over his ears, and he's bald everywhere else. How he put this garden tool up on the checkout counter, how he shouldn't have because he scratched the surface and nearly ripped at the rubber with the sharp instrument. How he made her stand there—For-Ever!! looking at him, trying not to look at him as he searched his vest pocket, his shirt pocket, his pants pockets, front and back—once more—because, as he told her finally, sheepishly, "I lost my wallet." And she'd already rung the damn thing up! Now what she'd have to do was call Frankie, the night manager, and have the whole transaction X-ed out—and really, it was just a few minutes before her break! Everyone was so nervous, I got so damn tense! and then she would stop because, there, she'd done it again, cussed in front of her little boy who was only eight years old.

Writing Prompts

What had happened for Dawn as she wrote? The story surprised her.

> I had started by writing from a memory, a fact, actually, and then created characters who moved easily into their own world, the realm of fiction. I knew these characters but didn't know they would be thinking and doing these particular things. Part of what gets them moving in any direction is the four elements; they gave me something to work with outside of my own memories or observations and a focus as I moved forward in the writing. As I wrote, the details of my own observations and thoughts connected somehow to the elements, showing me something about what I wanted to say and how to say it.

Working with the four elements guided Dawn in and out of her life stories. The prompt challenged her to make new stories, becoming a useful tool in Dawn's daily writing.

For others in the group, the four elements were too restrictive. We'd all felt the limitation of consciously trying to use all the elements just for the sake of using them and laughed at our frequently contrived efforts. In the beginning, it had been challenging to use all four elements, and many of us felt we were doing the exercise wrong if we didn't succeed in doing so. Once we discussed it, we felt freer to use them exactly as we wanted. We gave ourselves permission not to use all the elements in our writing, or not to use any of them.

If a prompt isn't working, find a way into your writing that will work. Dismiss the elements and move on. You may want to note what happens in your writing if you decide not to use all or some of the elements, but they show up anyway. Paying attention to how you use the elements may teach you something about your writing process, as it did for Dawn. Working from elements may reveal how much time you spend thinking when you write. It may show you that you don't need to think so hard in your initial writings, or that you want to be guiding them even more. The prompt may teach you about the elements of story like character, setting, or plot. And not only can it teach you, it may yield much useful writing, as it did for us. Our fragments—our name for these short pieces—have become studies for longer, more developed stories and poems, character sketches, and parts of novels. Some of them are finished and published pieces.

The List

We first tried the list prompt at the close of our second year together. We had been writing from the four elements for months and were open to a change that might lead to new forms for our writing. Someone suggested we choose a word, which we did informally, by calling out words and choosing the one that grabbed us, and then quickly write a list of ten words in response to it through free association. For our first attempt, we chose the word *statues*, wrote our lists, and then passed them to the person on our right. Each of us had a list of ten or fewer words to use as our prompt for the forty-five-minute writing time.

As we wrote our lists, we quickly shared our reactions. The lists seemed different from the four elements. For the nonpoets, the prompt was challenging because the lists suggested a response more like poetry than prose. For others, the idea of breaking from story was refreshing. Did we have to write poetry? Could we use all ten items on the list in our own freewrite? Would it be like using four elements? Would we *like* the new list passed to us?

The prompt invited us to try new forms. In the following pieces, for example, Jacqueline and Susan N. both created a kind of prose poem in which they delineated the sections by numbers. The excerpts of their pieces are preceded by the lists provided them in response to the word *statues*.

"Statues" by Jacqueline

statues
symbols
silence
liberty
"In memorarium"
anger
wall

1. I have invented statues for your pleasure. You must order, in either gold or white, and you may *request* male or female—but there we don't guarantee anything. Body parts, though, are a must. You understand, I'm sure.

2. There are symbols for everything I want to say these days—symbols lurking like shadows of oily men, of men with wet armpits who leer. The symbols keep crowding in on me. Some days, it's sunny out, but all I want to talk about are the dark clouds cutting across the sky.

Which is why I'm silent. . . .

"Statues" by Susan N.

statues
mesmerized
dictionary
golden apples
pears
surprise
infinity
stucco
barbarous
cymbals
Cochise County

I. In recognition of the barbarous acts of free will against humankind to perpetuate the freedom of the majority against the minority, the government of the white middle class erects this statue to commemorate the war just past.

II. In the statues by the water's edge, a stone woman gazes out to sea. Boys have placed golden apples at her breasts. . . .

VIII. Life cannot surprise a statue. They are mesmerized by infinity, looking through blank eyes. The dictionary does not help here. No words assault, clarify, contribute to an understanding of the stuccoed countenance.

Several of us wrote poetry that night, and others wrote short fictions, prose poems, dialogue, more lists. The lists became an invitation to explore form, and the more we used this prompt, the more varied our forms grew.

The list prompt also challenges you to collaborate and to free-associate images, places, and thoughts. With this prompt, start with one word, as we did, but for a future meeting try using other lists: for example, a grocery list, or a list of what you saw someone else buy in the grocery store, or your "To Do" list. You can give the list a theme such as places or people or song titles or food. When you free-associate, don't be afraid of the strange connections you may make! The writer sitting next to you has no expectations. Also, you need not use the entire list given you or write in any particular style or form. There is no one way to use this prompt. Like us, you may find this prompt pushes you into new styles.

Magnetic Poetry

We created the magnetic poetry prompt in the fall of our third year. It felt good to sit together after a long, quiet summer. We all felt the need to do what had always worked before, to simply write together—hard, fast, and willingly—and then read aloud. We wanted to create a new prompt to lead us there.

We were at Dawn's house. As we talked about possible prompts to use, Dawn jumped up, headed for her kitchen, and returned with a *Magnetic Poetry Kit*®, a small box filled with tiny magnetic strips of words. Instead of using the metal surface of the refrigerator, we sat on the living room floor and moved the chips of language around on the rug, forming sentences, fragments, and brief poems. Finally, we each put together one phrase. We could have written from the phrases we created for ourselves, but in keeping with our collaborative spirit, we passed them to each other to use as the prompt. Here are some of the phrases we created:

Picture these blue gardens wintering rust
through summer.
Cry whisper beneath all.
We sleep with vision next to you.

In the following excerpts, notice how our writing took many forms even though the magnetic strips suggest poetry.

Cry Whisper Beneath All
Cry is sharp on the end, a tack driven through sound, a shooting star, a comet, its tail lasting long after the initial burst of light and fire, anger and hurt. It is deep, Mammoth Cave, what's left when you jump off the peninsula of what they wanted me to believe was a quick route to China or eternity.

　　Whisper is the inside of my legs in slacks—hitting each other—passing by each other with every step. It is shadows on the wall from burning candles, shadows my kitty relentlessly paws, trying to catch them, trying to defeat them. Whisper is the smallest train whistle. Whisper are the words I say into Brian's back deep in the night. His back soaks them up—stops them short. He may dream someone else is breathing. Whisper is asking the hardest question (and not hearing an answer). Whisper is blue so light it's not Tucson July middle of the day sky—it's not Easter egg blue bonnets under cherry blossoms erupting along the Potomac in Washington. It's ballerina blue so

86

light, it doesn't hold up under the weight of Beneath. . . .

Dawn

Jacqueline received the line *Picture these blue gardens
wintering rust through summer*. She wrote a short fiction
that begins like this:

He actually said those words in his head, leaning
over the puddle of oil in the garage. A chink of
light through the window settled like the tip of a
flame on the thick liquid pool. He kneeled, not
young enough to feel healthy on his knees. He
kneeled because he hadn't prayed in many years,
and this moment mattered.

But he had nothing to say to God. In the
dark, near the wall shelves with dust and rusty
shears on them, he breathed, quiet and regular.
Picture these gardens . . . and he stared at the
pink and blue curling tendrils in the oil, and put
his face down, close to the oil, and he imagined
himself an Arab facing the Wailing Wall, kneeling
and kissing the ground. Slowly he lowered himself
into the lowest squatting position his legs could
manage, and then he looked over at the door, the
one that opened into the yard. The light was
green and black through that window, and he
could see the sky over the apple tree. He could
imagine Ruth walking past the door, heading toward the grill, no doubt—some place where meat
got cooked or Joseph or Alexandra had a scraped
knee to be touched with alcohol and covered with
a Band-Aid. . . .

One member wrote a sentence she created on her own, without the magnetic strips. Annoyed with all the tiny words and syllables, she threw up her hands and said, "I'm going to compose my own sentence!" (More proof that when a prompt isn't working for you, you can always find a way to begin writing!) She wrote, *He told me his secret to eternal life as we lounged under the orange trees in Monty's backyard.* Susan R. wrote in response:

> "It was just like Satchel Paige's," he said. "Never eat fried food; it angries up the blood. And don't look back, something might be gaining on you!"
>
> He smiled when he said that second thing but I knew that that was how he really felt, that the universe was really out to get him in the form of bankers, lawyers, clients—all those immensely important people who took up his time, ate his credit card lunches and kept his car phone ringing. The car phone in the Mercedes convertible paid for by the company, the company that had gone broke but not due to his management, oh no. Market forces, he said. An economic plunge.
>
> You, I thought as I stared at his reddish face dappled by shade from Monty's orange trees— you are reverting to the primitive philosophies of our ancestors. You don't cause things; things happen. Your company goes broke; must be a bad market. . . .

If you don't own a *Magnetic Poetry Kit®*, don't despair. Make your own kit of words out of paper or cardboard. Use nouns, verbs, articles, prefixes, and suffixes. Then, when you want to write, throw the words out on a table or on the floor and piece together a phrase or sentence.

Writing Prompts

Write from the one you create, or pass it to another group member. Once you get to know each other's voices and styles, you may even want to challenge a particular member of your group with a specific sentence. You may decide to create a phrase that suggests a plotline for a story, or one that suggests poetry. Notice that the prompt affects how a person responds. Dawn's prompt was so poetic and imagistic that it led her to play with language for the sake of language, rather than into a story or character. Of this writing experience, she says,

> When I read *Cry Whisper Beneath All*, it seemed I had two streams of thought simultaneously, and I jumped to follow them both as I began to write. I did not stop to think them out. One thought was to describe the words, and the first sentence I wrote was, "What do the words *feel* like?" And then, as I began to answer that question, the other idea defined itself for me. I asked, what does this whole sentence *mean*?

Jacqueline's prompt was also imagistic but more like a sentence, and yet it carried her into the beginning of a story.

We stumbled onto the magnetic poetry prompt because we agreed we wanted to try a new prompt. Do the same: Follow your instincts about your group and search for new ways to write together.

Working with Imagery

Pictures, images, visions. We see them as we write; we let them guide our writing. We don't question them, but are willing to trust what we see as they lead us to words, those sneaky, sticky syllables that slip out between the cracks, jump off the edge before we can stop them. But how often do we start writing from actual pictures, ones we see in a museum, in our best friend's kitchen, on a billboard along the interstate? How often do we ask ourselves, as we study the hollow cheeks of a woman sitting at a bus stop outside a drugstore, the lines, the angles of her face, the bench, the sign swinging in the dry southwestern wind, where the tension is, where our eyes focus, where the rise and fall occur? Who is this woman? Better yet, who does she remind us of? And what if we were to describe our own world in images, giving it not language but form, line, angle, color, depth, movement?

You may find, as Beth does, that starting with an image frees your writing in a way you haven't experienced and leads you to explore new styles, voices, and language. We have found these prompts to be challenging, fun, and sometimes intimidating, yielding intensely personal writing that is deeply imagistic and satisfying.

A Landscape of Your Soul

This prompt asks you to draw together, like freewriting, quickly and without reservation, and then to use your drawings as a guide for writing. For this exercise you draw a visual representation of your soul, your inner feelings about your life at the moment, a visual-''scape'' of your psyche and spirit. As with freewriting, this kind of drawing is spontaneous, so you can let yourself off the hook. It doesn't have to be finished or perfect. It just has to be.

You'll need large pieces of paper—any kind of drawing or sketching paper is good—and colored pens, crayons, pencils, watercolors, whatever medium your group wants to work with.

To begin, look at the blank page and ask yourself, what does my soul look like? What are its parts, and what are their shapes? Is it a literal landscape or a dream landscape? What are the colors of my soul?

In answer, draw for forty-five minutes, using the same guidelines as freewriting. Don't stop to think about where this picture is going, or if it looks like anything, or if it is good. Don't try to figure out what it means. Don't stop if you get stuck: keep your hand moving. The same subconscious process that governs your freewriting can also govern your drawing. Give into the act of drawing. Give your internal images external shape.

At the end of the forty-five minutes—and only then—label the parts of your landscape. Give the shapes, whether literal or figurative, a name. Susan N., for instance, called some of her parts "black and whiteness," "window of clarity," and "seaweed and sea of emotion." Dawn called some of her parts "thinking," "mask," "telling," and "listening." When everyone is ready to start writing, use your picture as your prompt. You can begin by listing all the parts of your landscape and go from there, you can begin by writing about the overall impression you get from your drawing, or you can begin by describing to whom this drawing belongs. The possibilities for writing are endless. You may find yourself going beyond the bounds of your image, as some story unfolds. Perhaps a single part of your picture will trigger a memory. Follow whatever impulse for writing occurs to you in the moment.

This prompt can take two hours to finish, so use the time well. You will want to read your writing aloud and share your drawings with each other. Many things may happen as you share your work with others. You may find wild or useless or perverse or lovely language. You may teach yourself and others something about yourself. You may see a character develop. You may find a new story. You may discover that you can draw after all! You may find that "freedrawing" before writing affects your writing, for better or for worse. If you're having fun drawing, for example, if you like the image you've created, how does it influence your work? Likewise, if you don't like your drawing, or if you can't let go and get started, or if your final product is dark and full of gloom, how does it affect your writing? Whatever happens, you'll want to talk about it, as we do.

We have found that drawing together may create more anxiety than writing together! Ask a group of women who fancy themselves artists of language to draw together and watch fear and embarrassment creep onto their faces. For one or two, drawing is always easy and fun. And some are doodlers. But for many, public drawing is a daunting task. Remember, there is no right or wrong way to draw this exercise.

When Jackie N. first drew her landscape in colored pencils, she created a lovely literal picture with hills, paths, flowers, a garden, a sky and sun, and labeled all these parts. As she showed it to the group and read her writing, Dawn wished she had the artist's eye to draw so convincingly. But Jackie said later that she thought she'd done it wrong when she saw so many other drawings that were simply shapes and colors, not realistic at all!

Jacqueline dove into her drawing enthusiastically, crowding her paper with layers of motion and color. Her writing is a three-part prose poem about the shape her life has taken. Susan N., who had done a previous landscape of hard edges and geometric shapes, wanted to try a softer approach and experimented with color. Her writing is like a private journal in which she discusses how and why she took this approach. Here is Jacqueline's writing:

1.

My soul has taken shape, here one large form unfolding, one bounded rubbing of color, surrounded by the tail ends of feathers, the shadows of someone in pain, the slow, centuries-long scream for life and eventual death of a river basin or a stand of trees somewhere without a human being in sight. Somewhere without a human form, I remember, there was a tenuous connection to life that began and continued, thriving until the balance shifted and the light from the sun overwhelmed the branches and bleached away the chlorophyll and destroyed the limbs down to the root, which finally rotted.

2.

My soul has taken shape beside the most confusing story that anyone has ever written. No one has chosen to write down this story. No one believes it is worthwhile to spend the decades it would take to pen each part and then go back and try to shape the pieces into a narrative. The plot metastasizes, the characters are a multitude, the task makes everyone tired, so that the gorgeous gashes of color in the story hurt their eyes and make their bellies cringe. It is like being too alive, inside this story.

No one has chosen to write down this story, probably because it is so simple. Some people's souls know this story. Some day I hope I might actually write it down. . . .

And Susan N.'s:

At first I drew horizontal marks of blue, green— my calming colors. The colors of nature: sky, trees, ocean, grass. I was safe, playing safe soul, as I do often, but I needed to rough it up. I put in some patches of red, then the top corner of purple (but it looked black), darker pink, orange, lavender. But I had then messed up the linear, calm, blue green fading to the horizon—serene as far as the eye could see.

My soul needed depth, color, shade, punctuation. On the bottom like a round patch of blue—now I began not liking the "linearness" of the colors: too many separate blocks of color—my worst fear—even if the blocks are green, blue— the blocks are solid, stolid, black and white, angular, stiff.

Motion, I needed motion, and then I remembered the wonderful St. Francis carving on the piano in the front room of Judy M.'s house with his slippery smooth lithe body, arms thrust upward, back curved into the ecstasy of the moment, a bebop St. Francis, the beat, the curve, the soul slink I wanted.

You may be thinking, "I just got up the courage to share my writing in a group, and now I have to draw?" You may start judging yourself and your abilities as a writer because you are uncomfortable with your drawing. Share these experiences and feelings with the group.

Writing Prompts

Talk about what's hard and why, what's easy and why. We have used this prompt only three times in the past three years, yet as our lives change, so do our souls and our soulscapes. We are willing to give them form again and again.

Cutout Images

You can also use pictures as writing prompts. One evening at Susan R.'s, we once again found ourselves searching for a new writing prompt. Susan R. went to her filing cabinet and pulled out a manilla folder filled with magazine cutouts, which she dumped onto the rug. There were color and black-and-white pictures of real people and places, reproductions of paintings, advertisements, sketches, and postcards. We each chose one or two prints and wrote for forty-five minutes. On another evening, we combed through Daphne's collection of *Harper's, The Atlantic Monthly,* and *The New Yorker* looking for images. Sitting in your host's house, look around and use whatever you see for a writing prompt: photographs, posters, paintings, calendars, wall coverings, or book covers.

Like the "Landscape of Your Soul" prompt, let the image guide you. You may begin by describing the image, its parts, its colors. Or the image may remind you of some earlier time or event in your life. Give the image a name and begin there. You can create characters based on the people in your image. You may also want to use the language accompanying the image as Beth did in one of her pieces. There is no set way to start: just follow whatever the image suggests to you.

Beth chose two dreamy black-and-white photos titled "Mara Floating" and "Flying—Porter Pond" by Andrea Gentl, which both showed a child floating above dark water. The photos had been printed with a story called "Video" by Don DeLillo, which is about a child video-taping a man being shot in his car on the highway. Beth says that as she wrote the following piece, if she got stuck, she'd find a phrase or word in the given text (the name Janet, for instance) to get her going again. These borrowed words or phrases are italicized in the excerpt below.

It shows a man driving a car.
It shows a second blur—
Mara floating,
Mara flying—
across Porter Pond towards the highway.
It shows the car drifting towards the guardrail
a *jostling*
a blur in the corner of the eye which is a
rearrangement of molecules in *the layers of* . . .
perception like tracking in a movie,
that blur when the girl who is holding the camera,
let's say her name is *Janet,*
shows us Mara floating, then flying
across Porter Pond, across two lanes of highway
and the man, who is *bald,* who is driving the car
notices only the haze of city lights in the distance,
only the moon skimming the telephone wires to
his left.
He notices that the moon and the car seem
to be stationary,
it appears as if the telephone poles are moving
beneath the moon,
as if someone is pulling a landscape along outside
the car. . . .

Writing Prompts

Susan R. chose an old birthday card showing two white swans, one grounded and one in the air, seemingly speaking to a red-haired young girl in a bright pink dress, sitting on the forest floor, a single pink flower in her hand. Her eyes are closed. Her head rests in the palm of one hand. Her feet turn in on themselves, almost unnaturally.

Susan R. began with what she titled "The First Attempt":

> She heard the honk and the flap of wings and she thought what a strange sound that is, like nothing I've ever heard before—the rush of wings, the electric rush, and she was overtaken, washed under by some force, sudden and magnetic. Oh no, she thinks, this can't be true, this is like some scene from a painting by the Old Masters. Some large velvety woman arched backwards by a magnificent swan. I'm not some damn mythological character, she thinks, I'm Rita Rosenberg and I'm a beautician and I grew up in Brooklyn. So get away from me, bird. . . .

Then Susan R. switched tracks and created a piece more like poetry. In this excerpt, she describes the image more closely:

> dreams are her natural element
> she thinks, holding a flower
> a flower that will soon die
> she minds, feels sad,
> reminds herself that all life dies
> including her
> the birds honk to annoy her

are they angels, she thinks
pieces of sky falling
or gods, disguised as Zeus was,
natural elements
she wants to give into them
feels trapped by her skin
the black of her eyelids
the leaf in her hand is a cool soft green
growing limp as it dies
but what dies exactly?
a lack of fluid? or is it some electricity?

To end the piece, Susan R. returned to the first attempt:

She's a beautician. She's done her hair herself, the red-gold tint, the perfect curls. And now it's being all messed up by these stupid birds. Are they serious about this? She is the superior species, she can just walk away. But every time she moves away they come closer to her, arranging her body to their liking, soothing her. This is where the magical transformation needs to take place, the puff of smoke. She waits, suddenly curious, to see what will happen.

Both Beth's and Susan R.'s pieces seem more like poetry in form, but we've all written memoir and fiction from this prompt as well. If writing from images works particularly well for your group, keep a folder with new and old images like you keep envelopes with words and the four elements.

Writing Prompts

Dreams

Dreams are a wonderful source of detail if we choose to write them down vividly and honestly, with vibrant descriptions and active verbs. In doing so, we practice describing landscapes, scenes, and images. We may not know how the pieces connect, but dreams give us rich material. If we wake up gasping, reaching for our notebooks in the dark to write at the first instance of consciousness, all we really need to do is remember those moving pictures in our minds and record them, wholly as we saw them. We don't have to think at all, except to say, I will not skimp on language. I will paint these images vividly. I will go for the jugular—which may be my own!

If you write out your dreams, you may find what you have are possibilities for future writing. Try writing out the dream you had last night, or the night before, or if you don't remember those, the dream you had last year. Can you remember the dream in which you were flying, fleeing, or searching for something? If you don't usually *remember* your dreams, write out the dream you *wish* you'd had. Or start with, "Last night I *didn't* dream about. . . ." In this way, you are not recording what you remember but using the notion of dreaming as a prompt. Ask yourself, how does telling myself this as a dream affect the language and form I create?

Trust this prompt. You may find it easy to fall into dreamlike narrative because our dreams, like rapid freewriting, tap our subconscious. Let the images of a dream, or even what the word *dream* suggests to you, get you started and follow where your writing takes you in a thirty- or forty-five-minute freewrite. Close your eyes, open your memory, and write out what you see.

Writing from Colors

It is a creamy off-white with a trace of yellow, and it is called "Honey Hue." It was once green but is now diluted, like dishwater, or white painted walls stained and dimmed by years of cigarette smoke, and it is called "Bone China." It is New York City in winter before a snow, and it is called "Stillman Gray."

These are the names of paint colors used by manufacturers to make their products more salable. The names are neatly printed under the colors on paint samplers, which are free, with no obligation to buy, at any paint store. They are a mine for writers looking for a way into their writing. The colors are usually printed on small rectangular strips of heavy paper. Have someone in your group collect about twenty-five of these strips and keep them in an envelope.

At your meeting, have each member choose a color strip. In response to one or more of the colors, make a list of images, memories, words, places. Use the names as well. (Stillman Gray could be a businessman, a famous actor, or a florist!) You can write from anything on your list. The possibilities are many. Perhaps the entire strip will remind you of a time, a place, or a person from your past. The point is to let the colors or names trigger your writing and go wherever they take you.

When you are writing, challenge yourself to use highly descriptive language. If you think of a sunset in Hawaii you watched with someone you were losing, how could you capture that sunset's colors without using colors to describe your feelings? Or how could you describe the fear, anger, and excitement just under your heartbeat in colors? What color is loss? What does the color "Hush Pink" *sound* like, *taste* like, *feel* like? How can descriptions using senses other than sight re-create the color of the sky?

Suggestions like these made prior to your writing won't interrupt your freewriting. You can decide to take your writing to another level even as you let the colors guide you to write spontaneously. Making the decision to push yourself may affect your writing considerably.

Jacqueline chose a brown color named "Sequoia." She did not describe the color, the word, or an image of brown. For her, the dark, rich color sample led her to a fiction about a pensive, brooding man who stained his fingers daily in a print shop, who dreamt of walking on mountains, in forests. Notice how indirectly the *idea* of brown permeates this excerpt:

> I am on a mountain thinking of the hawk's last trip the last time I walked uphill in my dusty brown boots, the last time I clenched my hands into small tight fists and felt my insides shudder, and watched the hawk swing low on her banking wave of air, so low I heard the feathers being riffed by the hand of God reaching down to touch me.
>
> I am not meant to be a medium. I never asked God to talk through me. I assure you these days, these long days standing in a stinking print shop, stale with musty inks pressed on metal plates, God has nothing to say directly to me. I hear a voice, low and intricate, like my mother's when I was a very young boy. I stared at her pinched face, her tightly clasped hands on her lap, talking on and on with the brown wall behind her, talking practically in tongues to one man, then another. Over the years, she was visited by a

few. I suppose now I'm grateful not to remember her specific words. Just the sadness mixed with yearning. Just the hint of pleasure behind the pain. . . .

Susan N. chose a strip of yellows. Notice in this excerpt how she wrote her impressions and comments to herself before settling into a piece, exploring the meaning of yellow with a density of detail.

Buttercup baby mayonnaise cocoa butter bop/ candlewick sonora oasis was a flop. The words ooze out like mayonnaise or cocoa butter—what is cocoa butter? And mayonnaise was never yellow except the few times I made it in New York, yellow haze of New Jersey over the Hudson. Yellow. (I should write color names like New Jersey Oily Orange or LA Smog Smear!) I've never liked the color yellow. The sun's shine is more white, clear, than yellow. Everything yellow is smudged dirty, nicotine stained. There. That's my new list for tonight: nicotine stain, cat pee—I'm lost. I can't even come up with lousy yellow words:
I am curious yellow.
I was curious, but yellow.
Old Yeller.
Yellow submarine.
Yellow bellow fellow caboo, I'm not writing much, are you?

Candlewick—the only candlewicks I've seen are blackened. At college I was taught never to put a candle on the table with an unburned wick. "Gracious living" at an eastern women's college. Were

we yellow? Too scared to let the candlewicks go
raw, unblackened? What would Edna St. Vincent
Millay say? Her candle burned at both ends—ours
at neither? But we did burn—in controlled, gracious ways. . . .

This prompt is an excellent way to push at your descriptive writing. The colors invite many forms, and every
time you use the prompt, challenge yourself to be more
outrageous, captivating, and fresh in your descriptions,
more dense, more intense. This will help you achieve
more original language.

Working with Characters

Grace stood at the mustard-colored door and
pushed the white round doorbell through the layers of unstoppable but undeniable memories. She
stood still, heard the chimes echo in the chamber
of that polished, empty hallway. Felt like Alice
about to take her step through the looking glass
and into a world of opposites. Everything backwards. The underbelly of everything showing—
seething and rising. What's beneath the umbrella
stand just to the left inside the door? What's behind the huge, gold-trimmed mirror hanging in
the main room? What lives under the potted
trees—under the rug—the floors, her own skin?
Maybe I should just walk in backwards, she thinks,
and get it over with. Still, she waits and looks down
at her protruding belly, normal as if she'd always
been a little overweight, but noticeable on her,
the slight one. They'll see. They'll know, she

thinks, and so what? Grace Blanket come home, come home to show them.

Dawn

What's in a Name?

There is only one way to find out: write the characters and let them tell you who they are. Beth first brought the idea of writing from names into our group. She came one evening with a list of names—Grace Block, Grace and Nola Blanket (from Linda Hogan's *Mean Spirit*), Gertrude Eastman Cuevas (from Jane Bowles's *My Sister's Hand in Mine*), and Temple Havendish. We chuckled as she read them aloud. Why do we immediately like or reject a name? What images does a name evoke? What characteristics, place, time, situation?

It is good to work with names because if you are a fiction writer, you will be working with character development. Your challenge will be to create a fully rounded character who could walk right off the page. Every time you work on your character, you will discover something new.

When you write in the group, use a new character name or write about a character from one of your stories, someone you are trying to get to know better. You can write scenes or sketches to bring the character to life. You are building an understanding of your characters that may or may not show up in a finished story.

Keep a list of names from your reading or your daily doings. Listen for unusual ones and jot them down. Use the names of real people, like Alonzo Mourning, the basketball player: look in the phone book, newspaper, or movies. You can even make names from objects in a room.

When you sit to write, you will probably choose a

name because of the strong image it creates. Don't stop to think too hard or analyze the character too much; just let your thoughts pour out. However, the following questions may help you get started:

- What does this character look like?
- Where is this character?
- What is this character doing?
- Whom is this character talking to?
- What is this character feeling?
- Who named this character?
- What just happened to this character?
- What does this character like to eat?
- When did this character last cry?

In the following excerpt, Beth began with the name Ruth Morning Waters; she'd combined Ruth Morning with one of Daphne's characters, Jocelyn Waters.

> Ruth Morning Waters: our mother, a small dark woman with deep dimples and black eyes which, if they are anything like her own mother's eyes, will fade to blue as she ages. When she was a girl, she lived in an old white house with a steep roof and turrets, on a ranch in California. She and her older sisters rode horses and wore blue jeans back when few women wore jeans. They wore their hair long and loose or long and in braids, braids wrapped up on the backs of their heads. The neighbors all thought of them as wild girls. Those Morning girls, they'd say, and shake their heads, as my mother and sisters flew down the dirt road in their father's model T, passing the steering

wheel back and forth and laughing, their hair fly-ing.

Ruth Morning, that's who she was, back then, before she met my father. That's who she was when she and her sister Nola held black umbrellas over their heads and jumped off the barn roof, hoping for flight. That's who she was when she decided to get drunk with Nola and Grace and poured herself a water glass full of straight gin, plugged her nose, and swallowed it down. . . .

Susan N. created her own name after several false starts one evening. April Mae Lickin jumped off the page, lending her snappy name to all the distinctive details in this excerpt.

April Mae Lickin liked her women strong and her men gone. Her father had left home one Saturday morning for Sharp's Hardware to buy a quarter pound of penny nails and never came back. April Mae figured he had pounded his way clear to Idaho by now, three whacks to a head, 180 nails an hour, 12 hours a day, 11,000 days ago. He must have spent a fortune at Sharp's, she reckoned. . . .

April Mae lagged behind, kicking stones and listening to the woods on either side of the road. In the woods she heard the sound of trees strain-ing under the weight of the sky, roots pushing against stones, leaves opening and closing to catch a breath. April Mae was more at home in the fields and woods than anywhere. After school she would head down Blackburn's farm road, swing under the fence at the curve, turn west and walk toward

Miller's mine. She would stop at the pump, rinse
her hands and mouth, and carry on. . . .

You should consider how the sound of the name
affects your writing and what it evokes. Without a doubt,
April Mae Lickin connotes a certain kind of person, different from Temple Havendish. You may also, of course,
work against the stereotype embedded in the sound of a
name.

The trick is to keep your hand moving. Try to flesh
out a character and make it real to you in your writing
time. Later, when you reread what you've written about
your character, you may want to write some more. Ask
yourself: What makes a character work? What makes a
good character? Write toward that goal. The group writing can be a valuable resource for strengthening your
sense of character, and group members can provide valuable feedback.

Extending Writing Together: Collaboration

By writing together, we are collaborators, in some
sense, sharing time and stories. In a way, we are creating
one text, even though we produce many, every time we
write from the same prompt. More than this, some of us
have been interested in writing texts together, intertwin-
ing our words with the words of other group members.
The possibilities for collaboration are many.

Passing Notebooks

Choose a word, sentence, or topic and write for ten
minutes. Then pass your notebook to the right. The next

writer will read what you've written and continue to write on your piece. The new writer can continue with your voice, plot, and setting or change the piece entirely. Everyone is still freewriting, still generating writing on the spot. You can pass as many times as you want, allowing reading time at the end, but try to write for at least forty-five minutes, passing notebooks at least four times.

We've marvelled at the stories and character metamorphoses generated by this way of writing, noting how another writer's view enlarges our own. When someone else finishes the story we began, we find out, much as our readers would, how the story ends, what our characters have done. We've laughed at the contrived plotlines and characters that emerge. Some writers may be possessive about a story, as if it had been theirs from the beginning. Others fail miserably at feigning interest in a plot or character they didn't invent. It may also feel difficult to start over so many times in one meeting. No matter. It's the exercise that counts, not the product. Use all the previous writing as a prompt for your own exploration.

In the following excerpt, the theme was "appetite." Susan N. began and passed to Jo Anne who passed to Dawn. Notice how certain words are picked up and carried on throughout the writing. Dawn had trouble getting started, so she quoted a line from Jo Anne's writing to begin. Borrowing lines worked as a prompt for her and in the end gave her a way to finish the piece. Using each other's language is fun and can be just the right inspiration. To borrow each other's language is a form of collaboration. In fact, as long as every member of your group agrees to do so, you can keep a running list of words and lines you hear and like in the group to use as prompts for your own writing.

Appetite. Sitting around this glass table eating crackers and writing about appetite. I think of a gaping hole, a mouth with rows and rows of perfect pearly teeth—canines, incisors, molars, wisdom. Well, no, not a gaping hole to be filled, to be crunched, bitten . . . no, appetite is more a yearning that won't go away, an emptiness, isn't it, no matter how much pot roast and potatoes and carrots one's mother cooks, no matter how large the turkey at Thanksgiving—I am actually reminded of Roma, Jeff's wife, at a Thanksgiving turkey sandwich party, with her hand in the turkey carcass, up to her elbow in bare ribs and limp skin, digging away at the stuffing, no piece not worth her.

Susan N.

Pot roast, potatoes, and carrots all together in one pot with crooked black handles, the one my mother used two, three times a week, our appetites back then were so simple, so repetitious.

Jo Anne

Our appetites back then were so simple, so repetitious. It was like the family was made of iron. *Our appetites back then were so simple, so repetitious.* Times of day were marked by mealtime. Sunday. Dinner at 2 p.m. Solid food one color of each. Each plate had an orange, a white, some green, something brownish. We sat quietly until Mother finished in the kitchen and at last the food was all on the table. We talked only on the surface: The meat is tender, the vegetables perfect, look how ripe the tomatoes are, we had a test in geometry. Mother wanted us

to tell her how pretty she was. But she talked of
tomatoes. It's as if the whole family were made of
iron.

Dawn

The process of interrupting yourself every few
minutes may be excruciating, or it may free you. For
those of us who have a hard time starting every time we
sit down to write, whenever we write, starting over every
ten minutes may be just what we need to break that writing block.

Pick-Up Sticks or Spontaneous Sentences

For this collaborative prompt, use each other's sentences spontaneously. Begin by choosing any prompt and
write for approximately ten minutes. After the first ten
minutes or so, someone spontaneously reads out the last
line she wrote. Everyone in the group immediately writes
that line into her own text and continues writing. Do this
at ten-minute intervals until you stop writing, after thirty
to forty minutes.

The results are wonderful. Often we've found that
the line given us is the exact one we needed in our text,
or it gives us a new direction that feels right. The line
may make no sense at all, of course, and you will need
to do what you can with it. Still, you don't have to use
the sentence as it is called out. You can choose to stick
with your freewrite without the intrusion of another sentence. Like the prompt "Passing Notebooks," this kind
of writing makes us pay attention and forces us to make
decisions as we write. Changing tracks at the dizzying rate
of once every ten minutes reinforces the spontaneity of
our freewriting, keeping us in the moment without think-

ing about what we are doing. We just see what rises to the surface.

The following two excerpts began with a quotation from a short story by Margaret Atwood. The italicized lines are the ones called out spontaneously in the group. In the first, nearly every spontaneous sentence seems to fit the story perfectly. When the prompt works like this, it feels like magic!

The second excerpt begins as memoir, and the spontaneous sentences seem to interrupt the writing. No matter. Remember, you can always follow where your writing takes you whether or not you use the prompt.

I.

"Cheerfulness was required at all times, even at breakfast." Marion was a night person. She usually slept in, over the time her Sony clock radio buzzed. She'd hit the snooze bar at least twice, every morning. On weekends she let herself sleep and sleep without a clock to interrupt her. Harold awoke before her and made no secret of his morning rituals. He peed with the bathroom door open, and then only half shut it before he shaved. Marion got into a useful pattern of ignoring him. She slept right on. He would be sitting at the table, neatly dressed and eating his dry, crunchy wheat toast when she rushed into the kitchen for a banana and a coffee to go. It all worked out for her. She figured she'd subconsciously planned to be late every morning so she wouldn't have to fulfill the requirements. *If she wasn't with him at the tiny kitchen table she wouldn't have to be cheerful. . . .*

Sitting in traffic, Marion imagines what happy cheerfulness without coercion is like. So it occurred to her, as she waited for a green light, that she could avoid Harold's sickening chipper attitude by not being there at all. Maybe she would simply not go home this evening, not sleep with him, not wake up to his oppressive presence beside her saying, "You really should get up now, Marion." She fantasized. It could be so easy, she thought, *and a smile froze like sticky wet candy on her face.* . . .

II.

"Cheerfulness was required at all times, even at breakfast." So it was, but really wasn't, in my family. My father, hardly full of cheer, more depressed, angry, grim . . . was especially loud and cheerful in the morning, his best time. He would wake early—I think now he was chronically exhausted—and make coffee in the same way, with the same motions, every morning. Always in the sink was a sponge with the same solitary streak of coffee grounds across the bottom third, mark of a single efficient swipe against some lip or lid of tin. My father would then take his coffee into the den and light his pipe—full of Sir Walter Raleigh tobacco—and blowing smoke and sipping coffee he would pour over his books—financial, personal, insurance. . . .

Much later in his life we knew he was sick because he started to reheat the coffee. . . . *If she wasn't with him at the tiny kitchen table she wouldn't have to be cheerful* . . . from the day before, he stopped plotting the natural gas consumption in the house that winter, and on the morning he died, an hour before his heart attack, he took out from his desk his will and laid it where my mother would find it.

My father was not full of cheer, but in the morning he was as loud and good as he got, and I—not unlike him in many ways—would creep quietly downstairs to retrieve coffee, silent, closed, and his . . . *a smile froze like sticky wet candy on her face* . . . booming voice would catch me with the usual "Good morning. How are you today?"

Even when a writing prompt doesn't work for you, we believe it's useful to continue writing to see what may surface.

Writing Prompts in a Bag

A rolled up portion of used Kodak 35 millimeter film; a photograph of a street in some town, mountains looming in the background, the sky a storm readying to erupt over the street you can't see because the photo has been torn in half; a piece of rosemary; a matchbook; an acorn; a piece of stale French bread; a soldier's medal; bougainvillea petals.

What do these objects have in common? Nothing until they are gathered by one of your writing group members and put into a small bag. On the table or floor where you write together, they are suddenly the objects of one character's life. When each group member brings a bag and hands it to another person, they are now the prompt for the evening's writing.

Imagine that all these objects belong to one character. They represent some part of the character, the things this character (whom someone else has really invented for you) would touch, see, use, feel, have in her or his life. Who and what do they add up to be? Your task is to write and find out.

We started using bags at Beth's suggestion, selecting objects we might associate with a person in one of our own stories. Because we did not write from our own bags but listened to how someone else developed our character for us, we learned something new about the people inhabiting our stories and took these insights back to our own writing. Like writing from names, this prompt leads to a richer understanding of the people created on the page.

Sometimes we fill bags with objects for an anonymous character. By the evening's end, we may have an idea for a new character, story, or poem based on the objects we received. The purpose of the exercise is to concentrate on what each item evokes, what memories it triggers, how it represents an emotional, intellectual, or physical aspect of a person.

Note how the objects listed below were used in the following excerpts:

I. by Susan R.

photo of girl on beach
koala bear
beads
leaf
bougainvillea
red lace garter
Colorings face powder

Writing Prompts

Johnson & Johnson non-stick pads
a postcard of a de Kooning woman

She sees herself at six, running along the beach,
the edge of the beach where the sand touches the
water, where you feel the water tug at your ankle,
your foot, trying to tug you in, pull you under,
under the waves. She was never afraid of the water, exactly, it was her element. She wanted to join
it. This is what scared her. She could imagine falling like a crumpled leaf and letting it take her,
take her, take her to the place where it was most
itself, where she could become herself. Isn't that
what we all are, she thought, no more than one
drop of water in an ocean. . . .

II. by Daphne

feather
card from vegetarian restaurant
whistle
pen

Behind the vegetarian restaurant was a small bird
sanctuary where Jocelyn sat on the cool stone, listening to the quiet rush of the waterfall beside her
and watching the solemn self-conscious peacocks
strut by, fanning feathers of a blue so strong, solid,
that it comforted her. If Hannah were here, she
would have tried to grab a feather from the dusty
ground for her; she would have risked scaring the
peacocks or getting bit, and Hannah would have
tried to stop her. . . .

Writing Together

crust of bread
black cherry lollipop
ruined, crinkled film
Utah pinecone
one side of a matchbox
bougainvillea petals
Air Force cuff links
peppermint leaf
rosemary
red pin
top half of a photograph, torn at the skyline in a
storm

Looking at the earth—only it's not there—looking every day at the sky as if someone had torn
the bottom half of the world away, all below her
sight line, Rosemary walked against the cold seeing only half of the world. Darkening clouds getting thicker like soup, gathering together
blocking out this already limited view. What did
she see behind her eyes on the inside? Another
unfinished scene, a night half lived, half done. A
single bed, too slim, for their roasting bodies.
Her roasting flesh. He had snapped at her,
when after it was over, she'd rolled up behind
him trying to mold herself into his form—
"Hot," he'd growled, "you're so damn hot,
back off," and she curled up into herself like a
roll of used up, ruined film, torn from the camera, never to be exposed. . . .

116

A Variation: Writing Each Other's Characters

Instead of using bags filled with objects, your group can help you to develop a character. As a group, choose to focus on a different member's story each time you meet. Read from some writing in progress, introducing a primary character. Then have everyone write for at least thirty minutes on that character. As your group reads, you may discover aspects to your character you hadn't known, or you may find ways to develop the character further because of things she or he did in someone else's writing. This kind of collaboration is obviously based on trust. Everyone writes to help another writer's work. Of course, each group member may enjoy the writing and take away something valuable for her own work.

Choose a New Style

By listening to each other, we have challenged ourselves to try different approaches to our writing. For example, some of us usually remain in the realm of autobiography when writing, whereas others write fiction. Over time, however, many of us found ourselves switching modes. To push your writing and your use of voice, plot, style, and form, one night suggest that everyone write in a style antithetical to her usual one. Purposefully try to write in a way to which you are unaccustomed, a way you've noticed other members of your group writing, a way that seems interesting and challenging to you. For instance, create a character of the opposite sex, try writing only fiction, try writing only poetry, try dialogue, try personal experience, try starting with a character or with an accident. Invent possibilities.

As a variation, write the names of your group members on slips of paper and have each member draw a slip. Then write in the style of that writer. Try to take on that member's particular style to see how it affects your writing. You may also choose a published writer and try to emulate his or her style.

Once you have been writing together for a while, you may have such a good sense of each other that you feel comfortable suggesting a particular prompt for one another. Choose a prompt for the particular writer to use, but don't say why. Simply offer the prompt and see what happens.

These prompts are excellent ways to force yourself past what is comfortable in your writing. If you commit to trying a new approach, one you admire or find challenging, you may take your writing to a new level.

Sustaining Longer Works

This idea came from our retreat (see pages 173–81). We were interested in supporting each other's longer works, whether we'd begun them in group or not. We decided to try this technique for several months.

Each of us brought pieces we were working on and read them aloud to the group. We discussed the strengths and weaknesses of the pieces and offered suggestions for how to proceed. Next, we all wrote for forty-five minutes on our separate pieces and ended by reading this new writing aloud. What usually followed was discussion about the direction of our pieces and ways for shaping complete stories and poems out of them. This talk was always useful and inspiring, a way to get immediate feedback on our writing approaches. What is interesting is that we found we changed *how* we wrote. We didn't all write quickly and freely. We read and thought and wrote and dabbled in thought again. Because we were all working on different pieces, at different rates, we did not share the energy we usually created when writing together from the same prompt. Still, this exercise is an excellent way to engage in the revision process because you can return to the same piece in the group as many consecutive meetings as you wish and because your audience is part of the process of writing as you create.

The prompts presented here may be experimental for you; they may push you to write in ways you've never explored. You can't foresee how your group members will respond to them or what each writer will gain from the writing. That's part of the risk. When you write together, write quickly and with abandon, and remember that at any time you don't have to use the prompt. However, be willing to try any- and everything as a group, always working toward finding exercises that are productive for each member as you work to meet your collective and individual writing needs.

Talking Writing:
Listening Well, Critiquing, and Speaking Up

5

I get such a sense of tingling and vitality from an evening's talk like that; one's angularities and obscurities are smoothed and lit.

—Virginia Woolf
A Writer's Diary

Although the original members of our group always intended to include the critiquing of each other's work as part of the group's process—and had strategies for doing so based on our experiences in creative writing programs and other writing groups—we rapidly moved away from this format to write together and read aloud what we had written. We chose to focus on freewriting because we were excited by what happened when we wrote together and found ways to respond to this work.

Anyone who has work to share, however, is always welcome to ask for formal responses. We learned we had to decide *how* to give those responses as more writers joined the group. When Dawn joined, she passed out copies of a story. At the next meeting she was disappointed when only a few members had written comments on her manuscript or had come prepared to discuss it. In the end, she realized some in the group had not even returned her copies! Dawn's disappointment is a lesson: you must discuss what you want from your writing group and define the "rules of engagement." In Dawn's case, we weren't trying to avoid giving the kinds of traditional responses common in writers' workshops, responses Dawn expected because she was participating in a workshop at the time. We simply had not yet decided how to give formal feedback. In our subsequent discussions about responding to our writing, someone suggested that we had to be sure about what we wanted from each other and then we would all try to meet those needs.

To avoid this problem, begin by asking everyone in your group, "What kinds of responses do you want, and what do you hope to learn from them?" Communication is the key. Early in the life of your group, whether you are novice or experienced writers, you should be making collective decisions about the following issues:

- How do you want to spend your time together?
- Will you focus on group writing and reading?
- Will you give informal responses to freewriting?
- Will you give feedback in a structured way to writing done outside the group?
- Will you prepare written responses to work, and how?
- What will be the role of the writer during response?

It is especially important to establish if and how you will respond in writing before you begin exchanging drafts. If you haven't participated in a writing workshop or group before, you'll want to think about how to write comments on your members' pieces:

- Will you write on each other's drafts? In the margin? At the end?

- Will you offer suggestions on elements such as character and plot?
- Will you correct or comment on details such as grammar and spelling?

You will also want to determine how the author is to participate during responses:

- Will she sit quietly and listen to comments about her work?
- Will she lead the discussion by asking questions?
- Will she discuss the process of writing the particular piece and what she intended with it?
- Will she ask in advance for certain kinds of feedback?
- Will she read her work aloud to the group or have someone else read it?

The answer is "Yes" if any of the above are what you specifically want as the writer during a response session. The bottom line is this: Define what you want from the feedback and set up your critique session accordingly. Everyone can choose for herself.

Our group's methods of responding cover a continuum of response techniques, one that has been mostly organic in its formation and progression. We arrived at purposes and strategies for responding out of our own changing needs. We began by focusing on writing and talking about what happened when we wrote, rather than on critiquing what got on the page. Then, although we believed that freewriting should not be critiqued, we found that many of us did want some kind of feedback: we wanted to hear what was powerful about the kinds of writing we were producing spontaneously. Clearly, some kind of informal response was the next step on our continuum, followed by more specific feedback on polished work.

Listening Well

If you choose to freewrite together in your group, one way to respond is not to respond at all, but to listen well. Essayist and poet Nancy Mairs says that listening hard is the best we can give any writer. A group that listens well creates a safe writing environment for its members because the purpose of the group is clear: it is not to critique, but to write and learn from the writing. The initial response to the writing, therefore, is an internal one: each writer experiences her writing anew as she reads it aloud. Reading to a group of people who are listening well is a kind of "response" the writer generates herself by paying attention to what happens when she is reading aloud. She learns from how she feels and thinks about her writing as she reads. Having the others listen well creates the environment for the writer to hear her words.

In our group, not making specific critical comments was a refreshing approach to our work together, especially for those of us who had experienced the negative criticism of some creative writing workshops. We did, however, receive a kind of response from the group as we read. We heard nonverbal signs of agreement, astonishment, recognition, regret, and appreciation, like sighs, laughter, deep breaths, and the occasional "hmmm" or "uh-huh." Body language, too, provided a response. We saw heads nodding, eyes widening. The group's responses were clear.

This response system offers several advantages. The safer we feel in the group, the more risks we will take in front of our audience. Also, by not soliciting formal responses, we are left to our own judgments about our writing. In our group we gain a sense of how our writing *affects* listeners, but we remain in charge of how we will become a better and more powerful writer. The learning comes from inside the self rather than from critical voices on the outside.

Informal Responses to Freewriting

Even so, we gradually wanted more. The issue for us was how we could respond usefully to freewriting without critiquing it. We moved into a more verbal method of response. We began to comment on particular phrases, words, and memorable moments in the pieces, still focusing on what seemed to be powerful about the freewriting. (Not every member speaks about every freewrite during each meeting, although some of us feel that no response is a negative one. These are issues you'll want to discuss.) In general, it is useless to critique freewriting because the writer has not made any choices or revisions yet. However, our format helped us move into discussions about what had happened for the writer when she was writing and what directions she could explore in further writing.

When responding to freewriting consider the following guidelines:

- Avoid talking about freewriting in terms of "good" and "bad."

Talking Writing

- Let the writer know that what she wrote made you feel something.
- Tell the writer what you remember most and why.
- Tell the writer what her writing reminded you of.
- Tell the writer what moved you the most and why.
- Tell the writer what language in the piece was powerful and why.
- Tell the writer what about her voice was powerful and why.

This kind of active listening and response avoids negative criticism, letting the writer know the *power* of her words, what is working and what is not. Every writer needs specific responses to her writing to improve.

You can also give this kind of response to work written outside the group. To get around the need to take writing home to be read between meetings, we often bring work to the meeting and read excerpts. We then discuss the piece, starting with members' initial responses. This process allows the author to ask questions and guide the discussion, based on what she wants to know about her work. This way, we get immediate response from listeners. Some members may take the piece home to write additional comments as well. Since the author receives comments at the initial meeting, she isn't disappointed if it takes longer than two weeks to receive other written comments. We also like hearing the work read aloud, as well as reading it in our own time.

Many of us expressed an interest in using the varied fragments we were producing in the group to write longer pieces (see pages 118–19). We decided to bring these pieces to our meetings and read several of them at a time for feedback. Again, we were interested in hearing our work read aloud, getting immediate reactions from listeners, and engaging in a dialogue about how to proceed.

Still, our feedback was informal. For example, Beth brought in a chapter from a novel-in-progress. She told us about rough spots in the draft, but she wanted a sense of whether the shape of the chapter was working. Jacqueline brought in some prose poetry and asked if each piece felt finished or if readers were left with questions. Dawn brought in a story she thought was almost done. Was it, she wanted to know, or was something off in the ending? Even with these direct questions, our group has decided not to use the formal critique strategies you will find in the next section. For us, providing informal response has been most fruitful.

If You Want to Formally Critique Each Other's Work

If your writing group chooses to critique work, there are productive ways to do this. We do not suggest you formally critique spontaneous writing, but rather formally critique only work done outside the group. Some general rules for effective critiquing follow:

When You Are Author
Know what kind of response you want to your work and ask for it specifically. Knowing what kind of response you want maintains your ownership both of your writing and

of its critique. If you want a critical reading of your work, ask for it. If you feel the piece isn't ready for an in-depth response, be clear about how you want members to respond. You can decide what is most helpful for you at any time. The more you write and share your work, the more you'll recognize when a critical reading is helpful.

Avoid telling everyone what your piece is supposed to do or be. You should not be altogether silent during the responses, but listening to what others have learned from your work is too important to be lost in self-explanation. As we state in chapter 2 (see pages 14–15), the traditional workshop model has the writer silent during the discussion so that she receives a "pure" reading of her work. You can respond after everyone has finished making comments.

When You Are Respondent
Speak right after a reading. Nothing is harder for the author to interpret than silence after a reading. Everyone should offer her first impression as quickly as possible.

Start with what is working in a piece. Begin all comments by telling the writer what's positive in her writing. No criticism should be less than candid, of course, but it is useful practice to find at least one thing that is working in a piece first. It's also good practice as a listener to determine what is good as well as what needs work in any given piece, since these issues may emerge in your own writing.

Be specific with comments, both positive and negative. Whenever you comment on writing, push yourself to be descriptive and detailed. "I thought the piece was good" is less useful than to point out specifically what makes the writing good. Is it the voice? What about it? What language made the voice believable? Try, "I liked the voice because . . ."

As listeners, you should be honest. Once you start by saying what you like about a piece, you then move on to a more critical reading, highlighting the mechanics of story, details, style, or voice. Your purpose is to help the writer learn something about her writing by explaining how dramatic, how convincing, how engaging the story is. It won't be helpful if you offer candy-coated comments that are not sincere. On the other hand, of course, it won't be helpful if your honesty is sharp-edged. Being honest in your responses can be tricky. Always focus on how you can be helpful. If something isn't working, try to be as clear as possible: "The voice isn't believable because . . ."

Remember: People have feelings. Everyone wants feedback on her work. But sometimes it can be hard to hear. Everyone comes to the group with her own expectations, tastes, skills in reading and writing, powerful emotions, and, above all, deep attachment to her writing. Each writer is on her own journey, which you must respect. Be honest and compassionate, clear and direct, helpful and informed when you respond to the work, but remember, no one learns much if she feels she is being attacked. And everyone's tolerance level is different. We have found that the safer we feel in our group, the better the critical discussions about our work.

If you are giving more structured, critical responses, naturally the intensity and risk increase. Many of us have learned from traditional workshops and from students in our own classes that it is easy to become negative when we talk about each other's writing. It is easy to tell the writer *everything* we think is wrong with a piece. Find ways to mitigate this overly critical response. After all, the purpose of the group is to support each other in our writing, not to "fix" every detail of a piece of work. The challenge is to find a balance.

*　　*　　*

In the traditional workshop model used in many creative writing programs across the country (see pages 14–15), writers distribute their works of fiction and poetry a week in advance, and workshop participants read and critique them for the next session. The goal is for the writer to hear critical discussion about the merits and weaknesses of the piece and to learn where she must work on plot, or character, or time sequence to get the piece working well. The benefits of this model, however, are limited if workshop participants are too critical, harsh, or inexperienced. In the hands of experienced writers and instructors, authors can receive a provocative reading of their work. Some authors in fact find it particularly useful to listen, even if they never converse, because the procedure gives them a critical distance from their own work.

If you want to develop a formal critique in your group, have one member distribute copies of her work at a meeting. Each member reads and comments on the piece outside the group and discusses the piece at the next meeting. You may want to follow the traditional model and encourage the author to only listen as her piece is discussed, or you may decide to have the writer lead the discussion based on her needs. Either way, we've found it most productive if the author takes responsibility for how the discussion evolves. The author may begin by asking a leading question about her piece or by saying something about the process of writing it. She might reveal that she wrote this poem more quickly than her others and is curious about its quality. Or she may say nothing at all. During the critique, members should give clear, direct, honest responses to questions such as:

- What is the movement of the plot and how is it working?
- Who is the main character? Is he or she believable? Why or why not?
- What is the voice like? Who is the narrator? Do they change?
- How does the writer use dialogue? Is it effective?
- How is time portrayed? Are there skips in time? Does the action move too slowly?
- Do you get a good sense of the setting of the story?

The following list, from Janet Burroway's *Writing Fiction: A Guide to Narrative Craft*, can be adapted for a group critique:

- What is the story about? What is the pattern of change?
- Are some scenes irrelevant?
- Is it original?
- Is it clear?
- Is it self-conscious?
- Where is it too long?
- Where is it undeveloped in character, imagery, theme?
- Where is it too general?

Talking Writing

If you want to formally critique nonfiction, consider adjusting the questions as follows:

- Is the point of the piece clear?
- Is the language precise and effective?
- Is the pacing appropriate?
- Is the idea fully developed?
- Is the tone appropriate for the subject?
- Are generalizations supported with enough concrete detail?
- Is the introduction lively? Inviting?
- Is the conclusion clear? Satisfying?
- Is factual information conveyed in an interesting way?

Think about what you hope to get from responses to your work and apply that to how you respond to someone else's. As respondents, we want to help the writer see her work more clearly. No matter what format your group chooses, the author should see the responses as constructive, supportive, engaging. By planning how you give responses, everyone in the group will understand the rules of the game.

What Writing Groups Talk About

Once you have read aloud and responded to each other's writing, you may find yourselves moving, as we did, into discussions about larger aspects of writing such as writer's block and publishing. And as group members relate their writing experiences, most likely you will also discuss issues of craft, including plot, voice, imagery, and revision.

This attention to the writing process mirrors what we do when we write together in our group. We pay attention to a subject and do not become frustrated when the word "hair" has us writing about the bristly beard of a man who kissed us a little too passionately when we were young. We don't throw up our hands and say, "Aaarrrgh! I wanted to write about my nostalgia for redheads!" We let our intuition, our right brain, our creative muse—whatever you prefer to call it—move us down the page. In the same way, when we talk about writing, we follow wherever our discussion leads us. Sometimes, later in the week, a group member will have a writing epiphany: an insight shared by another member during the previous meeting will untangle a writing problem.

When we began giving workshops on writing groups at the University of Arizona's Extended University, we were concerned about how to re-create the kinds of discussions we'd experienced in our own writing group because our discussions had been spontaneous and grew from the writing we did during meetings. We did not plan topics, nor did we assign responsibility for discussion to any one member of the group. However, to demonstrate to our workshop participants how these discussions could occur, we came up with an annotated list of some of our discussion topics. A few of these ideas may help your group start talking.

Writer's Block

"A sense of randomness," "fear," "being hypercritical," "an inability to swallow". . . . These are ways writers describe writer's block. You may suspect that if your group doesn't talk about writer's block, everyone (but you) is continually productive, and that bringing up the subject in your group will distract or even put off the others.

If you sincerely want to explore the issue of writer's block, be brave and bring it up in your group. You will learn that every writer has suffered from it at one time or another. Start by saying something like "I'm blocked. What do you do when this happens to you?" and stare directly at a group member you trust. Conversation will definitely follow. One or two in the group may claim they've never been blocked. "If anything, I need to learn how to shut off the flow of words from my brain to the page," someone once said in a workshop we conducted. The others wanted to throttle her. But moments later, as discussion ensued, it became clear that periods of writing paralysis and profound emptiness had visited us all.

The key to conducting a useful discussion about writer's block (as opposed to whining, sobbing, or philosophizing about it and then returning home even more frustrated) is to strip this subject of its power. In one workshop we conducted, we realized that it is the fear that the block will never end that causes misery, not the block itself. If we believe our ability to write will return, we are able to study our writer's block more critically and to learn from it. Blocks sometimes turn out to be gifts, we decided, because they tell us when we need to relax and to uncramp our writing muscles.

In *The Artist's Way*, a guide to increasing creativity, Julia Cameron urges all blocked writers and artists to ask themselves, "What am I afraid of?" Although our group members point to a host of different attitudes and emotions as the source of their blocks, fear is usually the root cause. For some, the fear of failing plagues and blocks the writer. Others may not know where to start. Still others fear they have nothing to say, or worry that what they write will not reflect the "brilliance" of their thoughts.

If you are plagued by fears like these, remember that it is always easier to think about what you want to write than to commit your vision to the page. Artistic visions change as you turn your ideas into actual writing, and it's a good thing they do. The halting way writing ideas evolve into drafts helps you understand the breadth and depth of your material. What started out as a nostalgic piece about childhood may begin to ring false because you need to write about something different. When a character is confusing, or a scene ambiguous, the writer may simply have to slow down, not necessarily grind to a halt.

Writing "hitches" such as these are not signals to give up. They may well mask real gems of insight. If you don't know why your character appears so wooden and her father so rigid in a scene you've just written, it's something you can explore. You may have found a new starting point or a new way into the complexity of your subject. By accepting your own slow pace, from inspiration and conceptualization through multiple drafts, you will learn to appreciate how each stage generates something worth keeping. You must admit that if you always knew exactly how to begin and end each piece of writing, you'd be bored to death. Creative writing needs time to unfold.

For all these reasons, we don't talk about writer's block as a "problem." It isn't. You will write again. You may be "empty," as Anne Lamott suggests in *Bird by Bird*. Your creative well may have temporarily run dry, and you will need to refill it. Lamott's "cure" for writing block: write your daily minimum of words on the page and then do something that inspires you. Walk through a garden. Reread parts of your favorite novel. Go for a hike at sunset. Visit a museum. Paint, sculpt, rake leaves. Cook. Eat well, and stay in the present no matter what you do. A good way to defuse writer's block, she says, is to live fully and without writing for a few hours. Observe the shapes of trees moving in the wind, smell the water in the air before a storm. Notice the wrinkles that have appeared under your brother's eyes. By taking in more of the world, you will have more to give to the page.

No formula exists for getting over writer's block. But talking in the group about what is hard in your writing helps. You will learn how others experience writer's block. Does it happen when they start writing? During the middle? How does it feel: frustrating? irritating? interesting? Do blocked group members slump in their chairs and wait for something to come to them? Or do they go off to a cafe, notebook in hand, in case the shadow passes?

You might want to try the "Writer's Block Metaphors" exercise in your group during your discussion of writer's block:

Write a metaphor for your personal experience of writer's block. Is writer's block a shadow, a black dog, or a shower of fuzz in your head? Describe an afternoon spent with this curmudgeon, this ball of ice, this genie—whatever you decide to call it. Make your language as descriptive and metaphorical as possible. Describe how the writer's block first appears to you. Does it look at you directly? Where is it located? How does it affect your mind and your body? If your writer's block has some-

thing to say, write down the conversation. Then share your writing with the group.

Reading these descriptions aloud will reveal how strong a hold writer's block has on some of you. Those who describe a mysterious and powerful force are probably more likely to feel overwhelmed by writer's block than those who conjure up a bullheaded, failed writer-turned-critic. Examining and laughing at your descriptions allow you to begin cutting your writer's block down to size.

During your talk, be sure to ask how each member breaks through writer's block. A member of our group uses the methods below to coax herself and her stubborn muse out of silence:

- Instead of sticking to the subject of the piece she's writing, she switches to one of her favorite subjects and writes on it for one and a half pages—no more. Then she turns to her original topic. She sits, breathes deeply, and finds that some of the momentum and creative energy has moved into her current project.
- She tells herself she must write terribly on her subject for three pages. Not one good idea can be included, or she has to start over. Often, she generates some good material this way.
- She turns her character into someone else. She says, "If this character were my mother . . ." and goes from there. She limits herself to a page or two.
- She meditates, then does housework as if her life depended on it. Ideas enter her mind as she cleans the stove and scours the sink.

- She writes in a journal about how terrible she's feeling about her block. Then she goes for a walk, studying shrubs, cacti, and the shadows on the mountains (focusing on nature keeps her from thinking about language). When she comes home, she is refreshed and ready to write.

Try these suggestions and come up with your own. You can report back the following meeting about how well these techniques worked to break a block or to break out of a rut (when your story drags and even your interest is flagging).

Recently, someone asked a panel of three distinguished writers speaking in Tucson if they had discovered any common thread among them. Yes, replied one, and it was the gratitude they felt knowing they were all writers struggling at this hard work at the same time in the history of this planet.

Realizing your membership in the world of writers may help you return to the desk with a clearer sense of why you do what you do and takes the fear (and some of the frustration) out of writer's block.

Voice

Sometimes our group talks about the writer's voice. We find it fascinating that so many writers—in our group, in our classes, and among our circle of writing friends—love to discuss this aspect of writing. Although we do not agree on a precise definition of voice, we understand it as the range of style, approach, and diction that uniquely characterizes a writer's work. Characters in stories and poems also have voices—if they don't, if all the characters sound the same, then the writer needs to

137

go back and make each voice distinct. But it is the first kind of voice, the style and type of content the author uses, about which so many writers talk.

Recently, we discussed voice with a group of mostly novice writers. They asked many questions: How does a writer know if he or she has a unique voice? How does one develop a distinct voice? Is it always the same one? That is, if a writer writes a story using a twelve-year-old narrator, and then a novel about four older women doing laundry at the laundromat, will the writer use the same voice in both works?

Writers give different answers to these questions in part because so many varied examples of strong voice occur in published literature. Some writers do indeed seem to use a unique style that sounds like that writer no matter what he or she writes. Others have a more varied repertoire, but each work they produce may have a strong voice. Members of our group admire writers whose voices can be easily recognized. A combination of confidence, color, and style lends their writing a distinct personality. The writer's personality comes through from behind the lines of text.

If your group is interested in exploring voice, read some examples of strong voice. Pick a story, novel, or poem and try to talk about what the author's voice sounds like. Jamaica Kincaid, Rick Moody, Jayne Anne Phillips, and William Faulkner are some authors we've talked about in our group. Although discussions about voice can become subjective, learning to articulate what *you* feel are the features of good writing will help you understand your own strengths and weaknesses as a writer. You may want to incorporate into your discussion an exercise that involves the writer's voice, such as attempting to write in the voice of a writer whose voice is distinctive (see pages 117–18) or using a sentence with a strong voice as a writing prompt (see pages 74–76). If your group writes together using lines from other writers' work as prompts, you may have sensed how powerful voice can be. When we used Cormac McCarthy's melancholy, lyrical line from *All the Pretty Horses*, "They stood and watched him pass and watched him vanish upon that landscape solely because he was passing, solely because he would vanish," as a prompt, many of us wrote more poetically than usual.

Most writers feel that a strong voice distinguishes good from mediocre work, but this is not the sole determinant of high-quality writing. What we call voice may, in fact, derive in large part from other features of good writing, such as clarity and specificity. The purpose of exploring voice in your group is not to fixate on it but to become more sensitive to what makes writing compelling.

"How Do I Know What This Piece of Writing Is and What Do I Do with It?"

Novice writers, in particular, often find that their most authoritative, adventurous voice is revealed in their shorter, more spontaneous pieces. Many of these masterpieces emerge during freewriting exercises like those described in chapter 4. Writers then wonder when and how they might develop these small gems into full stories, poems, or essays.

"How do I know what this piece of writing is?" is a question that comes up frequently in our group. One night during a group writing exercise, Susan R. wrote a wonderful vignette about a grisly redneck husband who every afternoon aimed his favorite hunting rifle at his beautiful wife when she was pruning their rosebushes. He said he was just practicing his aim. Using details adeptly, Susan R. placed this character in a time and place that felt real, frightening, and powerful to all of us. After she read her piece, we groaned with anticipation of the terrific story her piece could become.

Yet some of us are not sure how to develop a small piece of writing into a story. When Jacqueline brought in a collection of shorter pieces, she asked group members to help her decide which of the individual pieces were finished and which needed to be developed further. The group told her to consider gathering some of the pieces together and writing a short story made up of particular fragments. They found many of her other pieces "finished," however, and urged her to submit those for publication. The group suggested she consult editions of *Sudden Fiction*, collections of one- to three-page stories; Margaret Atwood's *Murder in the Dark*; and Karen Brennan's *Wild Dreams*, an award-winning short-story collection that includes short pieces of fiction, to familiarize herself with that particular form of writing.

The group also suggested that Jacqueline stop worrying so much about how to define her work—poems or short-short stories or vignettes—and concentrate instead on their content and on weaving the pieces together. Now Jacqueline is using scenes generated in the group to write a longer piece, and one of her vignettes was accepted by a poetry journal for what it was, a poetic meditation, complete in itself.

"How Do I Know I'm a Writer?"
After a reading, fiction writer Grace Paley, author of *The Little Disturbances of Man* and *Enormous Changes at the*

Last Minute, was asked which she liked better, writing or having written. "Having written," Paley said without missing a beat. Other writers in the audience laughed out loud, relieved to hear such a successful author admit this.

It *does* feel good to finish a story, print it, and mail it out to be published. It thrills us to show our story to friends and see and hear them respond to it with emotion. It doesn't feel as good to be halfway through a novel and stuck, or too busy to continue, or simply nowhere near completion.

Occasionally, our group talks about whether we feel like we are writers when we're not churning out polished drafts. Beth has had two different novels concurrently in the works, and at times her teaching responsibilities have kept her from working on either one. Susan R. hits dry periods while working on her novel, and Dawn struggles when she can't pull her vignettes together into a full story.

Writing *before* finishing is how you accomplish anything as a writer, we tell each other. Draft after draft after draft. A scene here, a tangential ten pages there that don't *seem* to belong to your novel yet but are connected to your main character. One truth about being a writer is that your work is more difficult if you don't enjoy the *process* of writing. Finishing novels, getting published . . . these are the milestones, but they occur infrequently. You must also appreciate and love the process of getting words on the page.

Writing takes patience and time for growth. You have to grow into your work and learn your subject. In our opinion, if you're writing regularly, then you have every right to call yourself a writer.

Submitting Work and Publishing

Most of our group have published stories or essays. Three of us have written unpublished novels and are actively searching for publishers. Four or five of us send new work out regularly. Sometimes in the group we talk about where we're sending our material, as well as how we feel about spending hours preparing manuscripts to send out, how we choose which literary magazines to send our work out to, how long it takes to get a response, and strategies for finding the one editor who will say, "Yes!" when coming across our work.

We know of a writers' group devoted solely to submitting work for publication. Members don't critique one another's work or write together. Instead, they read one another's pieces, talk about places that might publish them, and plan submission "goals." "You send this story to these five journals by next month," someone says. "You send three more stories to the editor who wrote on your rejection slip, 'I like your work. Please try again.' " Your group, too, can help members zero in on magazines that publish work similar to their own. Spend some time in the library or local bookstore reading through some of the many magazines that exist and collect information about potential publications to share with one another. (See chapter 7 for more on submitting work for publication.) Be sure, too, to talk to each other and to other writers in your community about how to start and continue this lifelong job of submitting work.

Members of our group generated this list of suggestions for making the submission process a little less painful.

- Particularly if you're just getting started at submitting (or are sensitive to rejection), submit work regularly to many different magazines and journals. You'll feel better waiting for responses from twenty-five magazines than you will sitting home wondering what happened to the single story you mailed to one magazine last week. Think of submitting as a lottery: the more you play, the more likely you'll win. Do not let yourself wait around to hear from one or two magazines. Submit to others in the meantime.

- Again, read magazines carefully and let your instincts and the submission guidelines steer you toward certain ones. Read the guidelines to learn if some journals publish work from writers living only in certain states, such as *ZYZZYVA* (West Coast writers only).

- Send a selection of poetry, not just one poem, and possibly two stories at a time instead of one. A grouping gives the editor more to choose from, and often magazines will accept a few poems by an author.

- As for sending novels or book-length nonfiction to agents (most agents won't represent poetry or short-story collections without the author having a novel published or in the wings, or many stories published), it never hurts to have a personal connection such as knowing an author represented by the agent. You can (with permission) write in your cover letter to the agent that so-and-so thought he or she might be interested in your work. You aren't being disingenuous or insincere by using these connections. All writers should have their work read by as many people as possible. Those with influence in publishing—published authors, editors, and agents—can give you guidance as well as help you get your foot in the door. They won't know you, of course, or help you get published unless you show them your work.

Experimenting, Talking, and Breaking Old Habits

In a university poetry workshop, an instructor tells student writers they must keep experimenting to survive as writers. They should write at night if they usually write in the day. They should start at the bottom of a poem if they usually move line by line from beginning to end. She tells them that using new approaches will give them access to untapped sources of material in their hearts and minds.

This is good and important advice. What we discovered by talking together about writing was that our discussions prodded one another to try things we would have never thought of on our own. Even the most committed nonconformists—those who write in bathtubs, while drunk, and when hurting with a broken heart— may not conceive of the experiments that will unlock their writing potential. Why? Because thinking up new approaches requires that writers step out of their own perspective. Even when new ideas are suggested, writers may think them too trivial and contrived to be helpful. Only upon hearing examples from other writers' lives will

144

an individual be persuaded to try breaking an old habit. To the highly disciplined writer, for example, taking a break from a challenging piece may feel like procrastination. Hearing other writers tell how much more gracefully they finished a piece after a long walk, however, can make a break seem like a good idea.

Talking about writing allows your group to become more than a place where writers get assistance with working drafts. Focusing on yourselves as writers, as well as on your work, balances the more technical assistance you provide each other, such as writing and critiquing. Members are not expected to "solve" each other's writing "problems," only to share them.

Sustaining a Writing Group
6 over the Long Haul

> So much of the satisfying work of life begins as an experiment; having learned this, no experiment is ever quite a failure.
>
> —Alice Walker
> *In Search of Our*
> *Mothers' Gardens*

Why do some writing groups meet month after month while others fizzle out after a short time? Why do some enhance individual writers' productivity while others produce too much conflict to be of any help? Long-term success requires agreement on core group issues, such as what members can expect and learn from the writing group. Sustaining a writing group also depends in large measure on the chemistry and creativity among group members, including how quickly trust develops and whether members continually find new ways to work together.

Yet no matter how carefully you've organized your writing group and planned your activities, no matter how sensitive and polite you are, meetings do not always proceed smoothly. Commitment, enthusiasm, flexibility, and honesty—key elements of successful writing groups—do not automatically follow when a group of people decide to get together to work on their writing. Writing groups join people engaged in the difficult craft of writing, and talking about their material is particularly challenging.

146

Sustaining a Writing Group

Two writers may speak in entirely different ways about literature. Their reactions to a piece of writing may be diametrically opposed. Because of this, you should expect disappointment and conflict as well as moments of intimate connection with group members.

In addition, we all live according to rhythms, to highs and lows, which for writing groups translate into periods of synergy and episodes of conflict. One night you may leave exhilarated from hearing members read their work aloud. On another, you may wonder if these are the same writers you met with the session before. Or someone feels down on her work, anxious about the future, and impatient with other writers. Frustration leads to silence during meetings or to prolonged disagreements about picayune details of a piece of writing.

Different leadership styles, timidity, or lack of trust may compromise your group's productivity. Moreover, outside forces—harried schedules and multiple commitments—continually influence meetings. Finally, the needs of writing group members change over time. The novel idea of working together may become routine. What worked during the first year—short writing exercises and lots of discussion about writing—may not work as well when most members are revising longer, more complex projects.

We have found that what threatens a writing group is also what the individual writer must overcome to succeed. On a near daily basis, writers cope with resistance, low energy, family responsibilities, the fear of failure, and competitiveness. These obstacles surface in writing groups as well. To survive as a writer—to call yourself a writer over time—you need both a thick creative skin and a willingness to change course midstream. Just as the writer needs to keep writing, despite anxiety and rejection, without becoming rigid, so must a writing group persevere with flexibility. Members need to recognize what isn't working for the group and then talk candidly about it. They must also listen carefully to other members' responses, even when they disagree, and find compromises. In short, successful, long-term groups have members who are open, flexible, responsive, and occasionally daring.

Focus on Writing

Perhaps the most important predictor of success in a writing group is the commitment of members to fostering one another's writing. By staying focused on writing, a group can avoid becoming bogged down in gossip, personal differences, fears, and organizational obstacles. In our group everyone wanted to write, read, critique, or talk about writing. Despite the fact that almost half of us worked together at the University of Arizona, we spent nearly all our time in the group improving our creative writing. When encountering problems, we avoided venting our anxieties or becoming personal with accusations. We conducted our discussions and meetings with seriousness of purpose. This doesn't mean we didn't laugh. We simply focused on our goal of improving our writing and remained determined to resolve conflicts so we could get on with our work.

Attendance

What Attendance Means to Each Writer

At times, attendance dipped in our group, particularly during the hot Tucson summers. When this first happened, no one viewed it as a problem. We recognized that all of us were busy, and we expected periodic absences. But a year and a half into the life of our group, as our size dwindled, we found ourselves feeling more like strangers than members of a group. At the start of one meeting, seated and ready to begin a writing exercise, Beth broke down and said what was on all our minds: We just didn't feel we had time for these meetings anymore.

So we talked about what made us skip or feel reluctant to attend meetings. The impulse began at home, before getting into the car to travel to the host's home, our minds spinning with chores, errands, assignments, and work we had "planned" for the weekend. "Do I really have time for this?" we asked ourselves, and a tiny, overwhelmed part of ourselves said, "Probably not." Group members had many reasons to think about skipping meetings. "If only my children behaved better," one person said, "then I'd feel okay about leaving them for group meetings." "When I get through this project at work, then I can clear my head and give time to the writing group," said another. Some reasons for missing meetings were more global: "If only my childhood had been happier."

At times each of us felt too distraught, overworked, underpaid, unhappy, or just plain tired to write. Whereas, in the early months, we looked forward to the protected writing time that our meetings promised, in its second year our group suffered from dwindling reserves of the faith, patience, and persistence writers need to keep from quitting. With time constraints and other responsibilities such as a career, relationship, or even a sport, writers will start reevaluating their writing lives, and the writing group is often the first thing they decide to skip "just this once," until their lives settle down. Although no one at our meeting wanted to quit entirely, we were each asking herself the same question: Am I really committed to writing, or am I just a dilettante, with a real life to get on with?

But missing meetings reinforces the fear and anxiety that overcome the desire to write. You may tell yourself you're just taking a break, when in fact you are letting your schedule determine whether you will get back on your writing track. In time, you may lose touch with the drive that compels you to write (even a few pages a day) no matter how busy you are.

Not that you shouldn't miss a meeting when you need to. Nicky's work on a film in Los Angeles kept her from coming to the group, as did other members' projects, but only temporarily. However, if the real reason you're skipping is that it's *hard* to be a writer as well as a parent, a teacher, and at least a part-time athlete, the consequences are more serious.

For us, missing meetings made writing more difficult. Some members told themselves they would do a marathon writing session on the weekend to make up for their absence on Friday night. When, despite their vow, they could manage only an hour of writing on Sunday evening, they'd feel terrible.

Your ability to handle the ups and downs of life and continue writing reflects your capacity to handle other creative challenges important to a writer. At our meeting, each of us recognized a familiar voice that complained about not having enough time for the writing group. The voice said, "So-and-so is getting published and is six years younger than I. I haven't worked on a story in two months. I can't finish my dishes, never mind that poem I started last week, so I had better skip the meeting.

150

When I'm relaxed and ready, THEN I'll give time to my writing group." That is, to your writing. You will treat your writing the same way you treat your writing group.

When we talked frankly about these attitudes, we learned everyone felt harried and struggled to find the time and the peace of mind to write. Our discussion taught us how to be more supportive of one another's anxiety and less critical when someone missed a session. We applauded ourselves when we showed up for a meeting, and we were more likely during the week to call those who'd been absent to see how the writing was going.

Honoring your commitment to the group, then, has more to do with honoring your commitment to writing than with not offending other group members. Attending meetings, even in the face of seemingly impossible obstacles, helps you overcome your resistance to writing.

What Attendance Means to the Group

When we first talked about our group's attendance, we focused on our individual reasons for skipping. We didn't consider how low attendance might affect the group as a whole. During the summers, when attendance frequently faltered in our group, we forgave each other for occasionally missing meetings. We still thought we were a strong group.

But in the fall of our second year, when the teachers in our group were burdened by a back-to-school crunch and attendance was lower than ever, Dawn brought up the subject of erratic attendance again. Because of it, she said, there was less continuity between meetings, less support, and less connection among members. Getting feedback on works-in-progress had become nearly impossible. When five members showed up one week, and only three of the five the following week, together with three "new" members, half the group hadn't read the piece and half of those who had weren't there to discuss it.

If attendance becomes a problem for your group—and it is a problem even if it troubles only a few members—then your group needs to find out whether members are dissatisfied with or somehow unfulfilled by what goes on in the group. A "Group Check-In" can reveal the issues that may be causing low attendance. We've used this exercise several times, most successfully when we are having difficulties in our group.

Respond in writing to the following:
(1) Why do I appreciate this writing group?
(2) I most enjoy coming to the writing group when . . .
(3) I least enjoy coming to the writing group when . . .
(4) What I want most from the group is . . .
(5) The specific change I think would most improve this group right now is . . .

After everyone reads her piece aloud, talk about the specific positive and negative aspects of the group experience that have been identified. Ask members to explain their preferences and dislikes. Discuss ways to highlight the strengths of the group and how to address members' concerns.

Successful groups depend on regular check-ins that fine-tune agendas and make meetings more useful. A variety of underlying problems may be revealed in your discussion of attendance problems, and you will want to address as many as you can. During our second year, for example, we talked about meeting on different nights every other week to accommodate different schedules.

"It's getting depressing when only three people call to find out which house we're meeting at," Dawn said. We were at her house, there were four of us, and we had to agree: when the commitment falters temporarily, it's better to meet less often and have fuller meetings.

Other options include a "must show" policy or a modified "must show" policy with allowances for members who call one another on a phone tree. In the latter case, the group can choose whether to cancel a particular meeting that promises a low turnout.

If your group is large enough, as ours was at one time with twelve members, a core of six who come regularly can keep meetings lively and productive. If the others attend sporadically, it won't disrupt the flow. Since writing groups evolve over time—as people rearrange their life priorities, learn to trust group members, and change their ideas about what they need from the group—you can eventually trust your group to reach equilibrium. As one writer in a long-standing group put it, the group "is what it is." If people are too busy, they won't come, and you can't change that by talking about it. Her group has a flexible attendance policy. Members don't get upset if some have to miss meetings.

The Reluctance to Participate

Participation in successful writing groups means active writing, engaged responses to members' work, and exciting talk. But in some groups, members hesitate to participate in these activities. Someone will ask, "What exercise do you want to do tonight?" and you'd think, from the blank stares around the circle, that she'd asked the group what color nail polish she should wear tomorrow. Otherwise engaged group members will fall silent when volunteers are requested to distribute drafts of their work. A member will ask how the others handle rejections from editors and no one will say a word. If your group is suffering from sluggish participation, consider the attitudes described below and be willing to talk about their presence among your members. Also, try the "Internal Dialogue" exercise on pages 155–56.

"This Is Like a Class, Isn't It?"

Some writers who are new to groups do not recognize that they are being asked to contribute more to a writing group than they might to a writing class. After years of passive listening in school, they act similarly in a writing group, observing and thinking but not speaking up. But a writing group is not "school"; it is more like a family of equals. Everyone must help make decisions, volunteer for activities, suggest new ones, and troubleshoot for the entire group.

Low Self-Confidence

Some group members' passivity stems from their low self-confidence about their writing ability. Like low attendance, poor participation sometimes reflects writers' diminished faith in themselves. They may feel their writing isn't "on a par" with the others' in the group, and so they hang back, afraid to expose their lesser skill. When called upon to read an exercise out loud, they pass, inhibition holding them back in their writing as well as in their group participation. When it's time to share experiences about writing, they discount their own, feeling they have nothing to offer.

To combat internal fear, writers must revisit the reasons they joined the writing group in the first place.

Sustaining a Writing Group

Members came together to learn and to grow. They joined the group knowing they would have to take risks and acknowledge their weaknesses as well as their strengths. To improve at writing, writers can talk about writing for only so long. They need to let others read and hear their work read aloud. They need to participate. In these ways, a strong group provides a sense of personal value to every member. Certainly, some may be more experienced or more skilled than others. But those who are less experienced—so long as they participate—are no less important to the group.

Fear of Exposure

Some group members hang back because they are unaccustomed to exposing their writing to others. Much of our writing is personal. Even the most fictionalized story reveals the way we see the world and, by inference, who we are and who we want to be. Sharing writing with the rest of the group can therefore be challenging, even frightening, for experienced as well as inexperienced writers.

Some writers feel they need to find special people to share their work with. Daphne, who joined our group in 1995, completed four years in graduate school, turning in paper after paper to her peers and professors, without finding a single person with whom she felt comfortable showing her poems and short stories. Even though she's an accomplished writer, it has been difficult for Daphne to share her work with others.

We suggest you do the "Internal Dialogue" exercise together and then allow those who feel comfortable to read their responses aloud. However, this exercise is *not* necessarily for whole-group appreciation, as some of the feelings that surface may be personal.

> *To acknowledge and honor the reasons you have not been able to fully participate in the writing group so far, try writing to the part of yourself that is quiet, shy, or afraid. Start by describing this part of yourself, either in second or first person (choose the one that lets you be more honest): "You are/I am quiet in the writing group. You/I feel exposed. You/I look around you/me at the other members and . . ." Next, ask this part of yourself why it feels this way. If no writing follows, ask this part of yourself what is so troublesome about reading aloud or speaking up during meetings. Then respond to what you've written. End your dialogue by discussing what you would like to change. Start small: "Wouldn't it be great if you/I told one personal story during the next meeting?"*

It isn't so important exactly *what* you write in this exercise but that you don't hold back. Say everything you need to say about your reluctance to participate. Venting these feelings may make them less inhibiting.

Troubleshooting Critiquing Sessions

Groups that choose to critique one another's writing need to insure that members are satisfied with both the style and substance of the exchanges. Certain kinds of feedback do not serve writers' needs. Feedback that is too vague or abstract leaves the author with unanswered questions. Worse yet, it causes the other group members to wonder whether *they* are going to get anything out of a critique from the group. We suggest you consider three potential problem areas for critiquing and formally address them with your group if necessary.

Sustaining a Writing Group

The "It's Not Ready Yet" Syndrome

Most writers want to polish the writing in a piece before they bring it in for feedback from the group. Some want to perfect it. They often promise to bring in their work "next time." But they keep finding more they can do on their own, and so they postpone the critique of their work.

Although it's a good idea to try to make a piece as good as possible for a critique, those who always claim their work isn't ready may be stalling—out of fear or perfectionism. They, too, need to revisit their reasons for joining the group, admit their fears, and push past them, submitting a piece for group feedback even if they don't feel it's quite ready. Such members need to realize that it may be helpful to check their perspective on their work, even if they feel it isn't done, against that of the others in the group.

If you've been working on a piece for some time and you haven't shown it to anyone, consider bringing it to the group for feedback. If you already have a plan for revision, you don't have to follow any of the advice given to you. But you may find yourself considering the group's insights later, when you're revising again.

Another consideration for the group is getting feedback at other stages of the writing process. The group may decide that it wants to discuss "unpolished" writing in addition to well-revised drafts. Certain slightly revised freewrites and rough drafts may benefit from a critique. Ideas for stories and notes toward poems can be shared as well. You can't take advantage of these possibilities for feedback in a writing group if you're unwilling to hand out work-in-progress that's raw.

Honesty

Incumbent upon groups that give feedback on members' work is that they give *honest* feedback. Presumably, the writer wants to hear the truth from you, wants to be told, although it may hurt, that her piece confuses, frustrates, or bores the reader, or that it is unfocused or unconvincing. If members of the group cannot or will not express their true feelings, then the author cannot learn anything. If someone cannot bear to hear the truth, she should reconsider bringing work to a writing group.

At the same time, it isn't easy to tell someone who has labored hard over a piece that it needs a lot more work, especially if she appears sensitive to criticism. For suggestions on how to give constructive feedback, review pages 126–27.

Even when following basic guidelines for critiquing, groups occasionally lose the thread of honesty, and their work together suffers. If you are the one not saying what you really think of a person's work, you'll feel uncomfortable during the session, and you won't look the author in the eye. Or you'll gush with praise for the effort and then, in your written comments, detail problems in the story you didn't have the courage to discuss in person.

But the author needs to know precisely what you think of her work. Force yourself to be specific: Say, "On page two, the character Jodie seems too lazy to clean and repair his mother's car after she comes home from her trip," instead of "Jodie isn't a believable character." Particularly if you find much in the writing unconvincing, try to say where and why its faults became evident.

What if you feel a member isn't being honest with her comments? The best policy is to say you don't agree and then give your comments. In workshops we've taught and taken, participants sometimes tiptoe around the truth until a brave person comes clear with what isn't working in a piece. After that initial criticism, the other participants join in and start telling the truth about their assessment of the draft. By being honest, therefore, you set an example for the rest of your group.

You need not worry about appearing contrary during a critiquing session, either. One of the best features of good group critiques is the debate among respondents. If each of you notes what you individually feel are the strengths and weaknesses of a piece of writing without delving into your disagreements, then you're likely to miss out on some of the most dynamic and helpful parts of critiquing. And sometimes, group members can help each other understand a member's work. Remember: the whole group learns from a critique, not just the author.

Falling into the "Right" vs. "Wrong" Mode

Groups sometimes fall under the sway of a particularly forceful member's critiques, but no one's opinion about a piece of writing is necessarily "right" or "wrong." Of course, the author may decide, after the critiquing session ends, that some comments were particularly thoughtful and therefore more valuable than others. But during the critiquing session, each member's perspective should be considered equally valid. The author needs to know what impression her words have had on each reader. She may find little use in most of what a particular member says, but a single insight from that member may be the one to improve her piece.

Jealousy and Competitiveness

Jealousy and competitiveness can threaten the support and encouragement writers in a group try to give one another. Sometimes, group members become envious of another member's success at getting published, winning prizes, or gaining group praise. Most writers remind themselves that in a world where thousands of stories, novels, and poems eventually get published, there's room for all group members to succeed. But sometimes it frustrates a writer to be one of the tens of thousands getting rejection slips. We forget to be generous and pleased for our peers; hearing someone else's good news, or even reading someone else's well-wrought poem, hurts.

Needless to say, competition will be destructive in a writing group. Not that envy can be entirely eliminated, but individual members can learn to adopt a perspective that keeps their envy under control.

If you compare your writing to another group member's and feel jealous, take some time to examine her writing more closely and try to learn from those qualities in it you so admire. Talk to the member about what she believes are the strengths and weaknesses of her work. You may learn that she, too, feels unsure of her writing ability or desires improvement in areas in which you are already competent. In this way, you'll see that the author is trying to develop her overall writing skills, just as you are. Try not to compare your successes to another's without recognizing that writers grow at their own rates. Comparing yourself with others denies this fact and becomes an exercise in self-flagellation.

Sustaining a Writing Group

When jealousy rages, it threatens a writing group's integrity. Someone will announce that her story has been accepted for publication in a certain magazine, and another group member will say she's never heard of the magazine or confide to other group members that she can't believe so-and-so's work was accepted.

In such cases, it's important to take a strong stand in support of all your fellow group members' successes. Say, "I can't wait until we *all* have our short-story collections out in hardcover." Smile and say, "So-and-so must have been thrilled to win a prize." Laugh at what seems to be random and unpredictable about success. Getting published, praised, winning, or simply feeling great about your work is a matter of luck and circumstance as well as hard work.

Leadership Problems

In groups with effective leadership, the mix of activities—writing together, critiquing, discussion, and so forth—flows well. Good leadership also creates a sense of continuity between meetings. Members leave with an idea of what will occur at the next meeting; absent members do not fall through the cracks.

Leadership, however, is rarely so effective. When no one leads, meetings drag on without direction. Or, when the group has drafted an unwilling leader, resentment may arise. The leader will dutifully initiate discussion, ask direct questions, even call group members to remind them about meetings, but without enthusiasm. Or a group may have a leader, not chosen by the group, who has "seized" control. Such a leader may cause dissension by dominating the group.

Annie, a poet in one of our workshops, described a leaderless group as awkward. After a writing exercise, the host would ask who wanted to read their piece, and when no one volunteered, the host would initiate conversation to which few contributed. Annie could see the exasperation on the host's face. Not eager to repeat the experience, Annie will no longer join a group without a designated leader.

If leadership is missing or misplaced in your group, we suggest you try a "Leadership Play" at one of your meetings. This exercise not only helps you see what's really going on in your group, but gets you out of your passive roles (at least while doing the exercise) and may get you to laugh at the situation.

> *Break your group into smaller groups of two or three and have each small group talk together about leadership in the large group. Then have each smaller group take center stage and act out a typical group meeting. "Actors" should not imitate particular members of the group but try to capture the flavor and pace of a meeting, highlighting leadership strengths and weaknesses. Use humor and exaggeration, but take care not to parody even a difficult group member. After each "performance," all group members, including actors, should write down their feelings about what was revealed.*

A writer told us about a group she paid to join with a well-known writer as its designated leader. Although the leader was both an excellent writer and critic, and the group was made up of "life or death" writers, as our informant called them—people who were determined to make it as writers—the group's commitment was challenged by the leader's style. Acting as a "prima donna," the leader wasted a fair amount of the group's time with self-indulgent theatrics. But since all were paying participants, the members learned how to give the leader some of the attention she seemed to need to stay focused on their work. In this way they handled what could have been a more trying situation and ultimately strengthened their group.

If your group lacks leadership, or if one member takes on leadership without being asked, we recommend that you experiment by rotating leadership either every meeting or every month. By taking responsibility for planning activities, facilitating discussion, and suggesting new ideas and approaches, each group member gains some valuable experience and an appreciation for how difficult it is to lead a group. The leader can try different kinds of start-up activities during her "time in office."

If your group still does not develop leadership, you need to find out why. You may need to open each meeting with a check-in to determine members' energy level, how excited they are about the ensuing meeting, and what in recent meetings has worked and not worked for them (see pages 152–53). Discussions like these may seem contrived, even difficult, but just a few can change members' perspectives about leadership. As you talk, you may discover that you have good ideas about what the group should be doing.

Other Interpersonal Issues

Writing groups suffer the same interpersonal strains as any family or organization. However, in a writing group, one cannot be transferred to a new division; nor can one "pull rank" or exploit the company hierarchy that puts one person in charge of another. In most writing groups, members try to treat one another as equals, which means basic communication and interpersonal conflicts have to be resolved by the group members themselves.

What obstacles stand in the way of comfortable group functioning? As mentioned, some group members may dominate meetings. They overpower the others by talking more often and more forcefully. You're lucky if your group has good participants with much to contribute, and talkative members tend to strengthen the group. But if the others can't be heard, you need to tell your "experts" to tone it down.

At times, writing group members may find themselves bristling. Someone is too harsh in her assessment of another's writing or makes a casual comment that hurts. What your group needs most is trust, so that when someone's comment rubs the wrong way, there is no breach of camaraderie. If you have grown and evolved together, then most conflicts will not become serious rifts. If someone giggles about a little boy outside the window doing jumping jacks while your poem is being discussed, then gets up noisily for a glass of water and actually has the nerve to ask, "Does anyone else need a drink?" well, you may be angry at the time, but you won't hold a grudge. However, if this person continues to act disrespectfully, then you, someone else, or all of you need to confront the "offender" and explain that her distracting behavior is unacceptable.

More serious is the case where someone in your group is abrasive, making sarcastic or hurtful one-liners that threaten the group's well-being. One thing you should *not* do is start complaining to other group members behind her back. Think hard, instead, about how to tell this person what's bothering you, and then decide how to approach her so that she's not defensive. For example, pulling her aside as she's on her way to her car after a meeting and saying, "I'm going to call you to discuss how badly you're behaving in the group," is going to give her something to brood about for days. Her defenses will be tough to break down by the time you call. Instead, invite her out for coffee, maybe sometime during the week. Talk to her about her writing, about yours, and about how you feel about the group. It might be important to her later, after she's heard you express your feelings, to know that you perceive the writing group as extremely important and helpful for your writing. Then, of course, tell her what's on your mind. Be honest and specific.

Unfortunately, the sort of interpersonal conflict that *does* harm a writing group is more subtle, subjective, and uncomfortable to talk about. Occasionally a person rubs you the wrong way, but there isn't anything truly wrong with that person's behavior, as when someone smiles and looks around the room, as your mother used to do, when she had something "difficult" to say. Even if this member has a penetrating insight about your work, you may feel uncomfortable because of her style of presentation.

You have a choice: leave the group or deal with it. Because we became good friends in our group, few truly divisive interpersonal conflicts have developed. We disagree, but we treat each other respectfully. In addition, our group talks mostly about writing together, not about each other's personality traits. Keeping the purpose of our meetings—writing—in the foreground helps us deal maturely with one another.

Jacqueline was in a writing group with a leader who one evening put a baseball cap on backwards and proceeded to pontificate about good writing. She demanded that everyone in the group stop writing precious, lyrical pieces and start "spilling your guts." This outburst, which lasted a good half hour, may well have annoyed some members. But everyone took it well. Whether they agreed with her perspective on writing, the members appreciated her passion. As Jacqueline remembers the incident, it felt good to listen to someone who cared deeply about writing.

Family Responsibilities

Surprisingly, one of the most persistent conflicts in our group concerns those we love most: our families. The four mothers in the group are frequently tired and taxed from finding baby-sitters, bringing their children to relatives, or knowing they will return home after a productive meeting to undone chores. Because our meetings are held on Friday evenings, a number of us feel impatient to get home and spend quality time with our families.

Most of us have had our commitment to the group "tested" by a loved one or child. Someone's partner will complain about not being able to go out on Friday nights or will demand to know in advance exactly what time the meeting will be over. These requests are often reasonable, but those who fare best at juggling family and writing group have made it clear to those involved the extent of their commitment to the writing group.

All members must negotiate with family members for their own time away. One way the group can make this easier is to have a fixed meeting time, allowing each member to make permanent arrangements for child care and the like. Another possibility is to find a sitter or willing child to watch over the younger children at the meetings.

Group members need to be sensitive to each other's family responsibilities. For one, try to choose a meeting time that is convenient and does not prevent members from spending important time with their families. Second, try to help out a member whose family responsibilities make it harder for her to participate. In our group, for example, Susan R. drives Beth to meetings so that Beth can let her son use the family car on Friday nights. Finally, if your group chooses to meet in one another's homes, talk candidly about whether a quiet meeting is possible at a home with children. Often it isn't, and the parents in the group will be relieved to not have to put unrealistic demands on their families.

Be sure to spend some time in your group talking about how to juggle family and writing. Lend moral support to the mother who steals a little time away from her family each week to write. If a meeting does extend beyond the agreed-upon time and a member cannot stay, be sure to call and tell her what was discussed after she left. Don't let her feel isolated from the group because of her family responsibilities.

Membership Changes

One of the best things—and one of the trickiest—that can happen to a writing group is gaining or losing members. New individuals are often the most enthusiastic members, bringing new vitality to writing groups. They are catalysts challenging, and sometimes threatening, the "old guard." Likewise, departures sometimes weaken the group.

Writing Together

Gaining Members

Many groups have difficulty deciding when and how to bring in new members. In our group, someone occasionally announces a local writer's interest in joining. Typically, the potential new member already knows that we usually write together in our meetings. A new member's willingness to do so is important for us because not all writers want to be involved in a process-oriented group.

For those who are interested, our door is usually open. The new member comes to a meeting and we follow our usual format. However, after one new member shared with us how it felt to join our group, we learned how we could introduce new members into our group more smoothly.

Jackie N. first heard about our writing group during a presentation we gave at a writing conference sponsored by the University of Arizona's English Department. Our group was a year and a half old. Writing together with others and then reading work out loud sounded challenging to Jackie N., so she approached one of our members about joining.

At her first meeting, Jackie N. found it a little frightening but rewarding to write with the others. A few months later, however, as she listened to group members talking about writing, she found herself feeling left out. Not excluded *by* us: she was there and could write, read aloud, and contribute just like the rest of us. But such a strong bond of friendship had developed among us that she still felt like an outsider.

These feelings are a natural part of being a newcomer. It is hard to come to a first writing group meeting and not experience the nibbling insecurities about whether you will contribute and be inspired by the others. What we learned from Jackie N., however, was that we'd neglected the courtesies of a thorough introduction, which would have helped her feel more welcome and would have allowed her and the rest of us to get better acquainted. From our discussion with Jackie N., we identified some simple procedures for welcoming new members into the writing group.

First, make your new member count. At her first meeting, ask her to explain her reasons for joining a group. Then talk together about whether your group will be likely to meet her needs. Such a discussion can inspire your group to new activities. For instance, you might learn that your new member doesn't know a lot about contemporary fiction and feels her work would benefit from a discussion of published work. Some of you could name your favorite authors and works and describe how you learned about the fiction you like: What libraries or bookstores do you visit? What do you consider the most important features of high-quality fiction? Your group could discuss whether it would benefit from a careful reading of published stories.

Second, at the new member's first meeting, review the group's progress. Share your individual reasons for joining the group, and discuss what is working well for your writing group—as well as areas for improvement. You could do the "Group Check-In" on page 152. Looking carefully at or reevaluating aspects of your writing group with the new member will help her get involved in planning the group's activities.

Third, recognize the value of enthusiastic new members. Ideally, a new member will suggest off-the-wall activities, ask direct questions such as "Where is everybody tonight?" and remind the rest of the group how exciting it is to read, write, and work together. Sometimes new members take a strong leadership role in their new writing group. In these ways they serve as catalysts for change, particularly for groups running out of ideas about how to work together.

At the same time, the high energy of such newcomers may take a little getting used to from the others in the group. Some groups haven't had a new member in so long, passion and enthusiasm are a shock. Certain members may not like the chaos a new member creates, particularly if she eagerly makes many suggestions and forces the group to confront its problems. Criticism from a new member may make older members defensive.

Adding a new member to your group changes it—and you need to be open to the benefits your new member will bring. Be willing to put up with some discomfort in the beginning, and be prepared to change.

Fourth, invite the new member to distribute some writing at one of her first few meetings. This doesn't need to be a critique; it's simply a good way for the rest of the group to begin to understand what she is trying to do on the page. If the new member asks for guidance on what to share, suggest she bring in a few different pieces—some older work she's pleased with (that she feels represents her writing style), and some work she's less sure about (perhaps the kind of writing she'd like to work on now).

The group can read the work and come back and discuss it or not: let the new member decide. She may feel it's enough just to have the others begin reading her work. The point for your group is to be sincere and open in its desire to get to know the new member's writing early on.

Fifth, give your new member a sense of the purpose

of each of your group's activities before doing them. Reassure her, for example, that writing done in the group is spontaneous and freely written and therefore will not be judged by the group. Tell her why you decided to do freewriting exercises in the first place and what your group members gain in these exercises. Such explanations and reassurances prevent the new member from being confused or overanxious about different activities. Indeed, the night we created "landscapes of our souls" (see pages 90–95), Jackie N. felt she'd created too literal a representation. She left that meeting feeling unsure of herself. Reassuring her that there was no wrong way to do such an activity would have helped her get to know our style more quickly as well as made her feel better about that particular evening.

Dropping Out

Just as a new member's participation will alter the makeup and chemistry of your group, so, too, will the loss of a member. A group member who leaves doesn't always explain why she is dropping out. The reasons may be related to the group, to her life outside the group, or to both.

Sometimes, there's just some loose talk about leaving and then the member drifts away. Sometimes, there's no warning at all; the member simply stops coming to meetings. One day a group member calls to see where the absent member has been. "I was just busy. I'll be there next week," says the absent member, uncomfortable about having to explain. As she hangs up she may think she will go to the next meeting. But whatever kept her from attending before continues to do so, and the group can only speculate as to why.

When someone leaves, especially without giving a

reason, a wound needs to be healed. It is a good time for a frank discussion about how well your group is fulfilling each writer's needs. When a group is on rocky ground—attendance is slipping and members are unenthusiastic during meetings—you need to talk together about the group.

When Jo Anne left, some of us knew it was because she didn't care to write together during meetings. She told another member she wasn't getting enough out of the group, and we didn't discuss her situation further. However, with hindsight, we should have. Other members shared Jo Anne's concerns. Ironically, after she stopped coming, the group talked about what we could do in addition to writing together. Members suggested many new ways to work at writing, but we had missed Jo Anne—she was already gone.

Leaving or Ending a Group

Writers, like lovers, sometimes grow apart. They have said and heard so much they have nothing left to share. When a writer reaches a point where she can no longer learn or grow with the group, it is an occasion to celebrate, not regret. The gains she has made by participating in the group have taken her to a new level, and she must move on.

At times even long-lived writing groups reach a mutual end. Groups that critique decide they would learn more from "fresh" readers than from the same devoted members. Sometimes, too, groups wait too long to troubleshoot their problems and become dysfunctional. Competitiveness, or too many unproductive meetings, may lead group members to call it quits.

Sustaining a Writing Group

When should you call an end to a group? When a critical mass of members believe there is no future for the group or resist efforts to improve it. If you talk together about the group and find that members lack enthusiasm and ideas and are unwilling to explore ways to change, the group may well have run its course. You can decide to stop meeting for a while and see if new members appear who want to revive it. Or, if some are still committed to the group, they can leave and let others continue. Even if your group was healthy up to its end, try to reflect on your new needs for a writing group and on what you want to do differently for your next group experience.

Staying Open to Change: The Writing Retreat

January 1995 was a quiet winter month in Tucson and an even quieter time in the life of our group. After two years of meeting together, our attendance had fallen off. No one complained about too much work or too many family commitments. In fact, no one even bothered giving reasons for absences or calling after they'd missed a meeting to find out where the next one would be held.

Ironically, this low period was preceded by a few heady weeks spent generating ideas about how to expand our group's work together. In October, we began talking about doing some collaborative projects, including a group reading and creating a large collage using our own artwork and writing. We also discussed giving in-depth feedback on portfolios of one another's writings, helping each other target journals and magazines for submissions, and holding a "submission-fest" where everyone folded, stamped, and mailed her new work out into the publishing universe in a frenzy of optimism and goodwill.

We wondered, after all those planned activities, why people were still not coming. And where was the enthusiasm that had gotten us through previous slumps? We decided an overnight writing retreat might answer these questions and reinvigorate our group.

A retreat suited our group better than a "special" meeting for three reasons. First, getting away from our families, friends, and jobs always encouraged our passion and excitement for writing as well as gave us designated time to concentrate on writing. An hour and a half drive away from Tucson meant a chance to nurture our creativity as well as our group. Second, rekindling our group spirit required more than our usual two hours together. Instead of trudging in on Friday evening, with dinner and the children's Saturday morning gymnastics lessons on our minds, we needed to spend a longer period of time together. Third, to get out of our rut, we needed to do something together besides writing and talking. We needed to see one another eat a meal, hike to a vista, and gaze at some mountains. We needed to breathe fresh air in a new environment to help us contemplate new possibilities for our group.

We decided against a four-hour drive to a lodge in the Chiricahua Mountains, as we would have spent too much time in our cars, and chose instead a night at a quaint hotel in Bisbee, Arizona, an old mining town turned arts community two hours southeast of Tucson. We'd have beds, bathrooms, steep winding roads, and trails.

Six of us made our way in two cars, arriving at the inn at eleven a.m. on a beautiful, sunny, sixty-degree Saturday. We laid down our books and bags in our suite of rooms, then shuffled a little.

"So what do we want to do?" Dawn asked brightly, but no one answered. In seconds, we felt fear seeping in . . . it's *hard* to define a retreat. It's hard to get started. It's hard to even take a stab at a plan when you're part of a group and you want all members to enjoy their time together.

"I want to write this weekend," Dawn said. We nodded. We knew we were going to write together. "But first, I want to do a little shopping," said Susan R.

"I'd like to hike," said Susan N. "Eat," came from Jacqueline.

We started laughing.

"I think we could split up—for a *little* while—without ruining our group experience, don't you think?" Beth said.

The rest of the day we broke into two groups and ate, shopped, hiked, and laughed. We had never done anything together before, we realized, except sit in a room and write and talk! After a dinner with the entire group, we returned to the inn and settled into an upstairs room with pens and notebooks in hand, ready to write.

Then someone suggested we talk a little about the group. "Our writing exercises aren't doing enough for me anymore," Beth said. This comment startled us— we'd been committed to those exercises for so long it seemed heretical to say anything even faintly critical about them. But she was not the only one to voice dissatisfaction with the group's activities. What the discussion revealed was that although writing in the group filled us with zest, it didn't connect well enough to the novels, short stories, and personal essays we toiled over at home. The process didn't seem as creative or exciting as it had in the beginning. Our eager creative community had fallen into a rut.

Jacqueline said she wanted to get back to talking about longer pieces. "I have notebooks full of promising beginnings," she said. "What I need to work on now, and what I want this group to help me with, is where to go next." In fact, each member had her own idea of what the group ought to be doing.

At first, this discussion felt like a blow to the group's spirit. Here we were on our retreat, and the group was in shambles. But talking about it, getting it out in the open, allowed us to see our many areas of agreement, our consensus about what needed to be changed.

We decided to postpone the rest of the discussion—how to deal with these issues—until morning. In the meantime, we would write, and the next morning, we'd talk again and make some decisions.

That night's group writing exercise turned out to be a marathon session—our longest ever. In our first exercise, each person created a list of words based on the word "mountain," as we were surrounded by mountains. Then each of us passed our list to the person next to us, and we wrote using as many of the words on the list as possible. It was an exercise that relaxed us and opened our minds. Why, for example, did "mountain" lead Beth to "cream cheese"? And what would Susan N. write from a list that included "solitude," "steam," and "haven"?

After reading and laughing, we returned to our suite and the two bottles of red wine that were stored there. With glasses in hand, we gathered in the biggest bedroom. After some chatting, Dawn picked a book off the shelf in the room and read out loud, " 'My relationship with Carl.' Start writing." Everyone laughed and hunkered down into her notebook. Afterward, we groaned from laughing as each person, reading her story aloud, started off with "My relationship with Carl . . ."

Then someone told a story about a garrulous uncle at the Thanksgiving dinner table. Throughout dinner the relatives kept telling him to "shut up." "Why don't we start with that? 'Shut up, Joe,' " Susan N. quipped, and off we were, writing again. By the time we read these, some of us were giggling so hard it was difficult to hear the words we read aloud.

This long writing session confirmed, particularly for those who struggled with writing together, that we were all capable of doing the kind of spontaneous writing that had excited us in the beginning of the group. It reassured those who fell into their writing stride toward the *end* of our regular meetings that much could still be gained from writing together. On this evening everyone had lots of warm-up time and lots of opportunity to let loose their creative muse.

The next morning, we walked up the stone staircase behind the inn to a covered patio on the hill. Under the canopy of elm branches, half in, half out of the sunshine, we wrapped ourselves in blankets, put on jackets, and sat together on rickety lawn chairs and a bench set up for meditative visitors. Rather than talk, someone suggested we write for fifteen minutes about how we felt about the group. After two years of working together, how were we doing? What did we want out of a writing group? Dawn says this was one of the most challenging writings she'd ever done with us. When it was her turn to read, she got right to the point: "I just want everybody to show up."

If she were really to write down how she felt, she explained, that would be the essence of her piece. The group meant a lot to her. "But for the last few months, when I go to meetings and only two or three or four others are there, it really affects my writing,'' Dawn read. Sometimes the group didn't even write together anymore. But it wasn't just not writing together; it was also that we weren't sharing our work. She missed that time every other week when she listened hard to other writers' voices. She had learned much about writing from those readings—as we all had—and now the group was letting her down.

After Dawn read, the floodgates opened. Everyone wanted attendance to pick up. Someone reviewed all the plans for new activities—the group's collaborative writing and reading, the art projects, the intensive study of how we revise. "I want to 'morph' the group," said Susan R. We laughed. We all wanted that.

Someone suggested we write on "morphing," or changing, the group. Exhilarated by the writing the night before, trusting one another because of the discussion we had just had, this freewrite, too, allowed each of us to share some of our deepest feelings about the highs and lows of the last two years of our group's meetings.

We also rekindled our desire to experiment more in the group. "I would like the group's work to be connected to the writing I am doing at home," wrote Susan N. "We could bring individual projects to work on— paragraphs, scenes, plots. Something that sounds a little disjointed to the group but not to ourselves. Or we could loop from week to week on our own work, carry on with a phrase or an idea from a previous week. Or bring a six-month project or story to do over the course of the time."

Beth, one of the more experienced writers in the group, with one novel written and another started, revealed that she is not willing to share certain work—such as her novel-in-progress—until she's somewhat distant from it. "At some points in the writing process, the novel feels too fragile to share," she said.

Someone suggested she could bring in an idea for a new scene, or read some of the earlier work from her novel that she's comfortable reading aloud.

"You don't even have to get any feedback if you don't want to," Jacqueline suggested. "But hearing your work helps all of us. And reading it aloud is going to help you hear your writing better. We won't critique anything unless you tell us to."

Beth nodded. That sounded good to her. She and Susan R., also at work on a novel she hadn't shared with the group, agreed that this new process might just work.

"I guess the question of the morning," said Beth, "is 'are we going to get married or not?' "

We laughed—because in a way it was true. Were we committed enough to re-create our group? To experiment with new approaches, to push the limits of what we could do together? Or had we waited too long and lost that commitment from each member?

We asked ourselves the same questions we asked two years before when we started working together: What are my needs? What do I want out of this writing group? Because enthusiasm had dwindled, and because we cared enough about the group, we talked on this retreat about our individual writing successes and difficulties and about what we liked and did not like about the group. We decided to try a few of our new activities over the next few months and to continue talking honestly about what was and wasn't working.

We went on a retreat because of a crisis in the life of the group. But on the way home, it occurred to us that a retreat should be a regular part of a writing group's life. Surely, anything that threatens to undo a group can be dealt with more fully at a retreat than at a meeting. In addition, if your group has changed membership, a retreat can help you get to know one another better. And if the group has decided to do some challenging, collaborative writing together—an extended group project, for example—you can devise a retreat to begin the new experience.

You can even meet other writing groups in a collective retreat and share ideas about keeping a group together. Just as hiking clubs meet for enjoyable outings, writing groups can learn a lot from swapping stories.

Looking back on our retreat now, we're surprised that it never occurred to us before to take ourselves out of our usual environment and talk and laugh and hike. Not only did the retreat bring us closer, but it gave us another view of each other, one that could only improve the encouragement, feedback, and advice we share about writing in the group.

Every group, every social organization, changes over time. Part of sustaining a commitment to any group comes with flexibility. Will you take a break from your group's scheduled activities to talk about one member's concern about child care? Can you spend time doing certain exercises or projects that aren't your personal favorites but are preferred by others in the group?

At the same time, for your group to prosper, you will have to speak up when you become discontent. Sometimes you will have to disagree with your peers. But if your group follows the spirit of this chapter, particularly by staying committed, enthusiastic, flexible, and honest, then individuals will be less likely to feel personally affronted by disagreements. Your group is a growing, changing organism. Discussion, troubleshooting, problem-solving—these necessary activities will keep your group vital and worthy of your commitment.

It is similar to what you do to keep your writing lively: you write, you read it back to yourself, and you listen for what is and is not working. Sometimes you gather information about the writing from others, in the form of feedback. You isolate the weak spots and either remove them or return to them with a new approach. In this way you don't coddle your first draft or keep moaning about what isn't yet effective. You refine and rework it.

In your group, try to agree on this ethic: We won't give up until we've tried everything.

Articles of Faith:

7 The Writing Life Beyond the Writing Group

All things human take time.
—Carolyn Forché
The Country Between Us

Working together in the writing group has made a difference in each of our lives. We have learned from each other, taught and shared and talked and listened. For most of us, the group has had a pivotal impact on our writing. The experience has enriched us all and will continue to engage us with hope and excitement.

Each of us sustains a writing life beyond the writing group, of course. It is to this life that we each return at the end of a Friday night meeting, some to darkened houses where we slide our notebooks on empty desks, lost in thought; others to children, lovers, and boisterous rooms filled with laughter, friends, and family. In some cases, our families beckon, eager to hear of the night's events. In others, their presence intrudes, as we would prefer to pursue a thought that arose barely an hour before.

We all have full lives, and a fundamental question for each of us is how to sustain our writing lives beyond the writing group? How can we use the group to enrich our writing, to return more ably to our personal artistic tasks?

Once you have established a comfortable relationship with an ongoing group, you will still need other sources of support and connection. It is one thing to write and complain and commiserate with a roomful of other writers. It is another to sit alone at your desk on a Monday evening and believe in what you are doing. How can a writer maintain connection to her work beyond the regular meeting with other writers?

Working with Group Prompts

If you write collectively in the group, the most obvious connection between the group and your writing desk is to develop what you have written in the group. You may choose simply to continue writing on the particular prompt, or you may find that your group writing provides new insight, power, and vision for something else.

After Dawn wrote in the group from a prompt with four elements—a pair of scissors, a campus preacher, a woman locked out of her house, and a Buddhist temple—she edited her work and later used it—entitled "Getting Dirty"—for an article in *WILLA* (Women in Life and Literature Assembly). She prefaced this piece with an edited version of something else that had come from the group: an essay we each prepared in our second year, describing what the group means to us.

Beth has used many of the group prompts to pursue ideas and premises for her second novel. Her piece on "shrines" was a variation of her novel's opening scene. The version she wrote in the group, however, was more directly autobiographical, and therefore closer to the emotional experience the word evoked for her. Her intention in the group was simply to get the experience down, not to use the experience to set up character or theme for the rest of the book, so she simply wrote about a shrine and a drive she had taken with her daughter and her daughter's friend. When she read this to the group, she was surprised that her voice went hollow, overcome by the emotion she felt. Her daughter had been doing something dangerous and probably told her about it only because one boy had been killed and another permanently brain-damaged in the incident. Even though Beth had already written about this as fiction, it wasn't until she wrote about it autobiographically and read the words aloud that she permitted herself to feel her own fear and helplessness. For her, this simple piece of writing had much more power than the fictionalized version.

Jacqueline has also used several of her writings in the group for her portfolio. When she does a public reading, she often reads several of the pieces, usually unedited and standing for what they are: short complete pieces that are neither part of a larger project or novel nor about to be turned into short stories.

Susan N. has used her writings in the group—mostly reflective, autobiographical pieces—to teach her something about her writing process. "Why this sudden concern with family, father, emptiness? Why this difficult time writing in a group, in taking myself and my writing seriously?" She has transferred insights from her writing in the group to reflections in her journal, her poetry, and her ongoing conversation with herself about writing.

The question of what to *do* with the writing from the group can be answered in several ways. You can simply keep writing, expanding on the material generated through group prompts, until you discover material or concerns that urge you to create a structured piece of some kind from them. You can decide not to write further, but to revise what you have written, fashioning it into something else—a short story, a poem, a prose piece. You can plug a newfound insight or language or character or scene into a piece of your writing currently under way. Or you can decide to do nothing at all, perhaps not now and perhaps not ever. You can simply let the writing stand for what it is—good writing practice.

With this last, of course, we have each come to realize that writing biweekly has helped us establish a rhythm to the way we each write. Even if we do nothing at all with the actual writing that emerges from our group work, we are always enriched by additional knowledge about how we write, like feeling reluctant to write quickly, like wanting every sentence to be perfect, like finding it difficult to abandon time-worn writing advice, like obsessing over our own autobiographical material. It is not only text that emerges from the group—language, characters, scenes, situations. We also take back to our writing desks the steady rhythm of writing for twenty or thirty or forty-five minutes or longer. We return home with the knowledge that we *can* write with passion, we *can* uncover important insights, we *can* fashion powerful language, and we *can* release our fears by suspending our critical faculties, by refusing to judge or belittle, by simply writing whatever comes out.

And we also return to our desks with new knowledge of how other writers engage their writing—Dawn's wonderful articulations about her writing process, Jacqueline's creation of stories whole-cloth, Susan R.'s ruby diamond from her soul map (which represents her writing self), Susan N.'s struggle past cliché, Beth's engagement with images rather than ideas. Writing we slowly understand is no more or no less than the transfer of energy, from our heads and hearts to the page, and from the page back again. A valuable knowledge of and belief in this process are what we gain from the shared writing in our group, well beyond the particular words we commit to writing on a particular night. And, in the end, it is this belief that sustains our work and ourselves beyond the writing group.

Using Readers' Critiques

If your writing group critiques previously drafted work, of course you will want to use the critiques wisely.

Your readers may think the piece is ready for publication, in which case, bravo! Or they may have read your work quickly or inattentively. In this case, it is up to you to decide if you need more feedback and from whom. But more likely, group members will have a lot to say about improving your draft. Again, bravo! Be grateful they have taken your work seriously by suggesting revisions and posing questions.

It takes time for a critique to make sense, so try not to rush home to make all the suggested changes that night. Sit with the readers' reactions and distinguish those that you understand and agree with from those that puzzle you. If you agree and see your way clearly, go ahead and make the suggested revision. Give your character a profession, red hair, a father-in-law, whatever seems to serve the purpose of the piece. If you agree with a comment but do not know how to incorporate the revision, let it rest. If the suggestion is an important revision, the needed change will come to you.

In some cases the comments and suggestions will be contradictory. Take the ones that seem right and work with those revisions first. Hold others that seem interesting but not completely clear. And feel free to set aside comments that seem entirely wrong to you. Perhaps the reader missed the point or was more focused on her concerns than yours. This happens.

After making these obvious changes, set the entire piece aside and return to it later with a fresh mind. Some of the comments may seem more incisive. But finally, of course, it is *your* piece of writing, regardless of what others may say, and you get to make the final revisions.

Try not to be discouraged by criticism. When group members are reading sensitively and seriously, they help you achieve more clearly what you set out to do.

Bringing the Group Back Home

Susan R. says she wants the group to be with her as she sits in front of her computer, sweating. Nicky realizes she is not as alone as she writes in her kitchen as she once thought. So as you sit to write on an ordinary morning, you can remember that a roomful of other writers are also sitting with you, cheering you on, listening deeply to your concerns and your language, helping you move the obstacles out of the way, rooting for you at every turn. Think of your writing group as a moveable feast, or at least a welcome party at your table.

Our group taught us the importance of scheduling a regular writing time, or times, for ourselves. Two hours a day before breakfast, two nights a week after dinner, an hour on Monday and three hours on Thursday—whatever fits, so long as you make it a firm commitment. Turn off the phone, pay bills tomorrow, prepare dinner in advance. Friends and family must respect this time, but primarily you must respect this time as reserved for yourself. Of course, don't twist your life out of shape to create writing time. Your life will always be more important than your writing, or should be.

So make a reasonable schedule, but then commit to it. It may be helpful to isolate your writing space—in a shed, garage, or rented room—to cut down on interruptions. Then show up full of faith and energy. If nothing strikes you to write, stay at your desk anyway. Don't wait for inspiration to sit down. Sitting down can be your inspiration. If you can't think of anything to write, write about that. Try to continue writing from a prompt you've already tackled in the group, or try various exercises from this or other books on writing. Describe your work area. Freewrite on an object on your desk, the feel of water on your face as you wash in the morning, the look of the house in mid-afternoon sunlight.

Many of us have found that it is important to remain nonjudgmental during these scheduled writing times. Go to the desk, put in your time, get up and go about your other business. Do not judge the amount "accomplished" in your time there. Do not count words, passages, pages, insights. You told yourself you would show up and you did. That is enough. You may have written brilliantly or not, copiously or not, painlessly or not. It is enough that you wrote. Over time your competence and pleasure will increase. Try not to judge how well the hour went, what you learned, what you understood, how it will play out in future hours or pages or books. Have it be enough that you wrote, and promise to return another day.

But what does this have to do with my writing, you may say, my intention to finish a poem or story and see it published? Everything. We believe that writing is not fundamentally about short stories, novels, poems, contracts. They may or may not come later. Primarily writing is about sitting at a worktable and moving your pen across the page, the cursor across the screen. And this absorbs time. And time is what you need to give yourself and then protect on a regular basis. And this takes faith—faith that you can sustain your schedule, faith that something will come of it, faith that you are engaged in significant, life-enhancing work.

Taking Notes

You may decide to keep a writer's journal. If you do, it will give you the pleasure of familiarity, a tool for concentration, a special personal place for your writing. Many famous writers have kept journals before you.

We will make a distinction here. A writer's journal is different from a personal journal. In a personal journal, you may describe your daily rounds or daily mood swings. You may whine, rage, justify, condemn. This often helps a writer keep her head and heart in balance. A writer's journal, on the other hand, is less indulgent. In a writer's journal, you observe the world around you. You may describe a scene that caught your attention at a red light yesterday—what Jacqueline calls "drive-by writing." You may try on new voices, describe old lovers, rant about taxes or the lack of social justice, describe tulips in May, re-create an incident from fifth grade, imagine a conversation with a cigarette, a bag of cookies, a crystal clear martini. And you need not only write. Save cartoons between the pages, paste in an image from a magazine and freewrite on it, draw or paint or scribble or scratch. You can create, explore, play. Collect scenes, details, images to use later in your work or simply for the practice of writing. But place no expectations on your journal—not even the requirement that you write in it every day. It should be a place where you can write freely, privately, wickedly or lovingly, depending on your desire. If you need help, a host of books are on the market to guide you in this enterprise. *The New Diary* by Tristine Rainer, for example, suggests several specific approaches to journal writing, as does Kay Leigh Hagen's *Internal Affairs: A Journalkeeping Workbook for Self-Intimacy.*

You may also want to keep a writer's notebook or small tape recorder by your bed. Dreams, with their easy access to our subconscious minds, have surprising force and clarity, especially in the middle of the night, so you may want to catch the rich vocabulary and striking images if you wake or when you first rise in the morning. Write quickly to record images before they fade, incidents before they disappear. You can always re-create your dream in your journal from the few telling notes you've scribbled in the fire or chill of the moment.

Anaïs Nin, famous for her journals, thought we mistakenly separate dream from daily life. She said, "Once I found that the dream was so interrelated with life, then I wanted to keep those passageways open and move from one to the other, not divide them, as they are really all one."

A notebook or small recorder in your pocket will allow you to make notes while driving around town, standing on line for a free bank teller, or waiting for your pizza. Did you read Sherwood Anderson's *Winesburg, Ohio* in high school? Were you struck by the image of Dr. Reefy carrying in his pocket hard wadded round balls of notes to himself ("thoughts, ends, beginnings")?

In fact, you can now begin—this very moment, since you are finishing this book—to treat yourself as a writer. What does that mean? Bonnie Friedman has an apt description in *Writing Past Dark*. She says,

> We are all bodies in the world, and our stories are the stories of bodies. To write meaningfully, we must grasp that. . . .
>
> We can do this: we can observe. We can take our pens and write what we see, what we hear. . . . People are incessantly expressive. . . .
>
> A writer's work, then, is to let us see what is being said. Daily life is always extraordinary when rendered precisely. We can unlock our lives with a pencil tip.

This knowledge informs and transforms every moment. No longer is waiting in line a burden: it is a gift, a small window of time in which to observe, wonder, soak up images, find language.

You can think of yourself as a "real" writer, because writing is simply using language to tell a story. You may work at your writing a little or a lot, you may succeed in ways that are publicly recognized or not, but in your simple desire to observe and use language, you transform yourself into a legitimate writer.

A Writing Partner

You may choose to work with a writing partner. Beyond the experience of meeting in a writing group and exchanging work or writing together, you may profit from meeting on a regular basis with one other person and writing together. Meet at a cafe, if you wish, or at home or in a park, but if you find a compatible soul, commit yourself to writing together at some regular time. The presence of another writer will help you focus, will help you take your work seriously, and will provide you with yet another audience for your words.

Read! Read! Read!

Of course, you will also need to read, read, read. Read fiction, nonfiction, essays, speeches, poetry. Read the old classics, read the newly discovered and the canonized, read contemporary work and the avant-garde. Read in your genre and outside. Read especially biographies of writers—heed their struggles and learn from their mistakes, fortitude, and faith.

You may also profit from books on writing and creativity. (We list numerous titles in the back of this book that have been important to us as writers.) A host of good books are on the market. Older books like *Becoming a Writer* by Dorothea Brande and *If You Want to Write* by Brenda Ueland were written in the 1930s. Common sense never ages. Newer books like *Surviving a Writer's Life* by Suzanne Lipsett and *Writing Past Dark* by Bonnie Friedman speak eloquently about the life of a writer.

Other books like *Bird by Bird* by Anne Lamott and *What If?* by Anne Bernays and Pamela Painter offer specific instruction and advice on writing. Classic books like *The Artist's Way* by Julia Cameron contain important insights and guidance on nurturing your creativity in general. Books like *Walking on Alligators* by Susan Shaughnessy provide sound advice and daily inspiration. Once you become a writer, you become part of a community of creative artists whose stories are your story, whose struggles are your struggle, whose victories are your victory.

You will want to hang out, of course, at your local library and favorite bookstore. Libraries are amazing because the books they have are free, and they are willing to lend them to you! In these cost-cutting times, they may not have recent best-sellers, but they often have wonderful old out-of-print titles. (Try to find Dorothea Brande's *Wake Up and Live!*, the story of her personal enlightenment written in the early part of this century.) Meander through the stacks of the library or peruse the sale tables at bookstores. Often books you will cherish are the ones you encounter by happenstance. You might use one book to spark interest in another. So much of our reading has been directed in school: try reading directionless for several months, letting one book suggest a new train of thought or an interesting sequel.

Subscribe to literary journals, book reviews, and trade magazines such as *Writer's Digest* or *The Writer*, two monthly publications with articles about the craft of writing. Join Poets and Writers, a New York City organization devoted to promoting writing and writers, and receive *Poets and Writers*, a bimonthly magazine highlighting the legal and social concerns of writers as well as profiles of authors and announcements of grants and awards. Subscribe to a variety of fiction journals such as *Sewanee Re-*

view, Ploughshares, Granta, and *Grand Street.* Read reviews in magazines such as *Belles Lettres* and *The Women's Review of Books* (both devoted primarily to writing by or about women), the *New York Review of Books,* the *New York Times* Sunday book review section, and *The Atlantic Monthly, Harper's, Saturday Review,* and *The New Yorker.* Look also for several collections issued yearly: *Prize Stories: The O. Henry Awards, Best American Short Stories, Best American Essays,* and *Best American Poetry.*

Be sure to attend as many public readings and lectures as you can. Local bookstores, libraries, community colleges, and other organizations frequently arrange readings for local celebrities or visiting authors, and sometimes the author will also speak about the craft of writing. Writers in the flesh are always entertaining and provocative—if only to complain about their hard lot!

All these suggestions will help you engage the writing world on a personal level, day by day. Move at your own pace, learn simply and grow deliberately, but feel free to make the world of language and literature your own, because as a writer in a community of writers, it is.

Classes and Workshops

You might also be interested in taking a writing class at the library or local school. If you are weak in any of the basics of writing—grammar, syntax, vocabulary—this might be a good time to face your particular demon and wrestle it to the ground. More enjoyable might be classes or workshops on journal writing, fiction, poetry, the short story, the novel. Often the instructors in these classes are productive published writers and have a lot of good advice and hard-won personal tips on how to improve your writing. And you will meet other like-minded students in these classes, with their own goals and writing lives to share. You may find, as we did, that your community is full of talented and generous writers, willing to share their knowledge and enthusiasm.

Beyond your community, you might wish to sign up for a weekend workshop or retreat in a neighboring city or state. *Poets and Writers* has frequent notices of these workshops. They may specialize in one genre, such as poetry or writing for children, or simply feature one or two guest speakers with more hands-on activity included during the afternoons. Looking to increase the use of their facilities, many colleges and universities around the country have summer workshops or for-credit courses you might wish to attend. They, too, feature well-known writers in all genres and a chance to have your manuscript read and critiqued by a professional.

You might also consider enrolling in a college degree program. You can major in creative writing as an undergraduate, or, if you have a degree, you might consider returning to graduate school in a fine arts or literature program. Although this is no small-time commitment, you may find just the encouragement, instruction, and camaraderie you seek. Your local library can provide you with lists of schools that offer such programs.

Sending Work Out

Writing is a business as well as a personal and spiritual pursuit, of course, and at some point you may decide to approach the publishing market. The library is an excellent source of materials on the business of writing. Be sure to look for a series titled *Writer's Market* published by Writer's Digest Books. (Other titles include *Poet's Market, Children's Writer's & Illustrator's Market,* and *Novel and Short Story Writer's Market.* Look for the one that is right for you.) These books provide a general overview of the writing profession and a thorough description of particular literary markets—book publishers, consumer publications, trade journals, and other areas broken down by category such as religious, mystery, and romance. The listings provide names of editors and publishers, addresses, telephone numbers, general description of the business, and preferred manner of submission. These guides are published annually, and library copies are usually up-to-date. Also valuable is the *LMP* (*Literary Marketplace*), an annual compendium of information about the book publishing industry, including book publishers, agents, printers, and awards. Finally, you might consult *Publishers Weekly,* the trade journal of the book industry, which contains news, articles, announcements of upcoming books, and reviews.

As you perfect your craft on the one hand, you need to hone your business skills on the other—that is, if you plan on sending your work out. Ah, sending your work out. How hard that is! How debilitating! How important!

How important is it to you to send your work out? You can write every day of your life, take immense satisfaction from it, feel the generosity of its rewards, and never send a single word out for publication. On the other hand, you might be fiercely single-minded about being published. You might feel that none of your good work and honest thought will mean anything unless you have the opportunity to share it with others, to communicate your observations and ideas. There the search for legitimacy begins, the march toward public acceptance.

If you decide to send work out, do your homework first. Choose an appropriate market for your poetry, short story, article, or novel, using the reference books mentioned above to avoid sending a romance novel to a science fiction house. Better yet, read previous issues of magazines and journals, or survey the kinds of books a particular house publishes, before sending your work to them. In fact, most large publishers do not accept unsolicited manuscripts, and many journals and most publishers like query letters first, explaining the nature of your proposed project and describing your background and ability. Often they prefer that you be represented by an agent. (Again, the library can help here with books like *Guide to Literary Agents, How to Write Irresistible Query Letters,* and *How to Write a Book Proposal.*) If you get a request to submit your work, prepare your manuscript properly. Proof the material carefully. Enclose a self-addressed envelope with proper postage in case the manuscript is returned. Be neat. Be friendly. Be humble.

But be determined. If the manuscript is returned to you, send it back out that afternoon. Sometimes multiple submissions—submitting the same piece to more than one party—are acceptable. Be prepared for a hundred rejections if need be, but take heart: *Gone with the Wind* was rejected nearly twenty-five times before it was accepted for publication. (*Rotten Rejections* from Pushcart Press provides much solace to writers by reprinting rejections sent to famous authors such as Nabokov and Le Carré.) Keep large envelopes by your desk as well as postage and a scale. They, too, are the accouterments of a working writer. Log in the dates you send your material out and to whom, and when manuscripts come back, update the list.

But whatever your ratio of acceptances to rejections, rejoice! You are a writer in the world.

Just as necessary as inuring yourself to public rejection, of course, is steeling yourself against public acceptance. Nothing is more joyful, or fleeting, than the fifteen minutes of public recognition Andy Warhol promised us all. We want your piece, they say, and you are off to the races, a wild and woolly ride. Not that it's all bad: those of us who have been published would not trade the experience of seeing our work in print, of having readers, for anything. We knew our work was good all along, but after the tumult comes the silence. Where are our fans? The television spot? The contract? The cash? Often, even after several publications, fiction, poetry, and memoir writers end up as we began, at our writing tables on a particular day in May, listening to our inner voice for guidance and wisdom. Tell me what to write, we say, and a small heaving stirs inside.

In addition to sending manuscripts out, you may also enter literary contests. Contests may have cash prizes, and they certainly carry prestige. They usually have specific requirements: a word limit for a short story or a line limit for a poem. They will direct your energies for a time and help focus the work you are doing on craft.

Another way to keep yourself going is to write your favorite authors and tell them you think they're swell or disagree with a lousy image or extend an insight. Susan N. once wrote the poet Maxine Kumin to complain that one image in a poem—that of the sun "oozing" into a summer sky—didn't work for her. Kumin was generous in her reply. And Dawn, deeply moved by *Surviving a Writer's Life*, wrote author Suzanne Lipsett, quoting lines she especially liked and telling her why. Lipsett wrote an appreciative letter in response. At the Pima Writers'

Workshop in Tucson one spring, author Gregg Levoy mentioned—in a talk entitled "The Business of Writing"—that he always keeps a drawerful of postcards, paper, envelopes, and stamps by his desk ready for a quick note. Keep in touch, in other words. Most writers like to receive mail. It extends the dialogue, enlarges the felt audience before a writer at his or her work area.

And then there is always that very writerly public pursuit: lunch. Commiserate with other writers, complain about the children, lambast the publishing world, discuss an image, worry the definition of a word. Go public with your enthusiasms, your trials, your victories and defeats. Sharing the burden will lighten your load, and talking honestly with other writers will renew your energy and faith in the business of writing.

Finally, as a reward, every month take a writer to lunch—yourself!

Sustaining the Writing Life

It is clear to us in the group that we have managed to sustain the writing life beyond the writing group largely on faith, hope, and charity.

We bring faith to our writing, to the rightness of our pursuit, to the significance of writing, to the evolving growth of our talent and accomplishments, and to the purpose behind our language. It is fundamentally important to have faith in *your* writing life.

It is fundamentally important to believe you are a writer, for so you will become. Do not think you will become a writer once you fix this or alter that, do not think you will become a writer when the kids leave home or the laundry is done, do not think you will become a writer tomorrow or next week or next year. Believe you are a writer now.

Beyond faith, we also have hope: hope in our lives, in the life of the group, in the rewards of writing, in our growth, and in change. We have hope that our writing will evolve, our understanding will deepen, our words will signify and stick. We have learned to support, encourage, open, change, and grow.

Society so often portrays writers as isolated and alone, with disturbed or disturbing visions of society. We have found the opposite: it is through community and shared experiences that writers best realize their individual humanness. Writing is not competitive or comparative—contrary to popular belief (for example, the single awards, rankings, polls, and best-seller lists). The poet Adrienne Rich once accepted one of her countless awards on behalf of every writer. All writing enlarges us. This is our life, and we can only tell our story, walk our path, tell the truth about what we know. Know that this is enough. This is the hope, the promise: that your writing life will be transformed from the group experience.

The charity we feel is simply the generosity we extend to other writers . . . and to ourselves. Recognize that wherever you are in your writing is exactly fine: you are constantly learning, growing, changing. Do not wish to be someone else. Wish to be what you are at the moment fully. Do not seek to be better without a willingness to work, of course. But be aware that effort is sufficient. It is not beyond your grasp. It is our belief that writing from the heart, finding words for our experience, is an essential act of living and creating.

Guide to Group Exercises

from Chapter 3, "Getting Started"
Ideal Writing Group   54
Core Group Issues   55
Defining Individual Needs   57
Exchanging Work for the First Time   58
Exploring the Writing Process   59
Sharing Writing Models   59

from Chapter 4, "Writing Prompts"
Working with Words
    Words   67
    Sentences   71
    Impromptu Prompts   74
    The Four Elements   78
    The List   82
    Magnetic Poetry   85
Working with Imagery
    A Landscape of Your Soul   90
    Cutout Images   95
    Dreams   99

Guide to Group Exercises

Writing from Colors 100

Working with Characters

What's in a Name? 104

Extending Writing Together: Collaboration

Passing Notebooks 107

Pick-Up Sticks or Spontaneous Sentences 110

Writing Prompts in a Bag 113

Writing Each Other's Characters 117

Choose a New Style 117

Sustaining Longer Works 118

from Chapter 5, "Talking Writing"

Writer's Block Metaphors 135

from Chapter 6, "Sustaining a Writing Group over the Long Haul"

Group Check-In 152

Internal Dialogue 155

Leadership Play 162

Good Books for Writers

These are our personal favorites, books that have opened our eyes to other writers' experiences, guided and instructed us in our writing, and uplifted us when we needed inspiration.

Allison, Dorothy. *Bastard Out of Carolina.* New York: Dutton, 1992. A young girl survives her abusive childhood in the south. A National Book Award finalist.
———. *Skin: Talking About Sex, Class and Literature.* Ithaca, N.Y.: Firebrand, 1994. Allison writes about how she started writing her real story, despite the pain.
Anderson, Sherwood. *Winesburg, Ohio.* New York: Viking Press, 1960. A fictional portrait of an American town.
Atwood, Margaret. *Murder in the Dark: Short Fictions and Prose Poems.* Toronto, Canada: Coach House Press, 1983. Vibrant, scintillating short prose pieces by a master.
Baker, Sheridan. *The Practical Stylist.* 7th ed. New York: Harper & Row, 1990. Basic instruction on good writing.

Bernard, Andre, ed. *Rotten Rejections*. Wainescott, N.Y.: Pushcart Press, 1990. Former rejections of the now rich and famous.

Bernays, Anne, and Pamela Painter. *What If? Writing Exercises for Fiction Writers*. New York: HarperPerennial, 1990. Eighty-three exercises with clear instructions, objectives, and examples.

Best American Essays. New York: Ticknor & Fields, annual. Best essays of the year.

Best American Poetry. New York: Macmillan, annual. Best poetry of the year.

Best American Short Stories. Boston: Houghton Mifflin, annual. Best short stories of the year.

Bishop, Wendy, and Hans Ostrom, eds. *Colors of a Different Horse*. Urbana, Ill.: National Council of Teachers of English, 1994. Creative writers who also teach examine the creative writing classroom.

Bowles, Jane Auer. *My Sister's Hand in Mine: An Expanded Edition of the Works of Jane Bowles*. New York: Ecco Press, 1978. A collection of well-wrought work.

Bradbury, Ray. *Zen in the Art of Writing: Essays on Creativity*. Santa Barbara, Calif.: Capra Press, 1990. A master of science fiction describes the delight and wisdom he brings to writing.

Brande, Dorothea. *Becoming a Writer*. 1934. Reprint. Los Angeles: Jeremy P. Tarcher, 1981. Julia Cameron calls this "the best book on writing I've ever found."

———. *Wake Up and Live!* New York: Cornerstone Library, 1936. Brande's personal insights into achieving success and well-being, noted half a century ago.

Brennan, Karen. *Wild Dreams*. Amherst, MA.: The University of Massachusetts Press, 1991. Winner of the Associated Writing Programs Award for short fiction.

Bryan, Sharon, ed. *Where We Stand: Women Poets on Literary*

Tradition. New York: W. W. Norton, 1993. Twenty-two women assess their relationship to gender and poetry.

Burack, Sylvia K., ed. *The Writer's Handbook*. Boston: The Writer, 1995. Covers basic information for writers, writing techniques, and marketing.

Burroway, Janet. *Writing Fiction: A Guide to Narrative Craft*. 2d ed. New York: HarperCollins, 1987. A superb guide to writing fiction.

Cameron, Julia. *The Artist's Way: A Spiritual Path to Higher Creativity*. New York: Jeremy P. Tarcher/Perigee, 1992. A twelve-week guide to recovering one's natural creativity.

Cather, Willa. *Willa Cather on Writing: Critical Studies on Writing As an Art*. Lincoln: University of Nebraska Press, 1976. A collection of letters and essays on writing.

Chatman, Seymour. *Reading Narrative Fiction*. New York: Macmillan, 1993. Narrative theory applied to traditional and contemporary short stories.

Children's Writer's & Illustrator's Market. Cincinnati, OH: Writer's Digest Books, 1996. A helpful guide to publishing children's literature.

Cool, Lisa Collier. *How to Write Irresistible Query Letters*. Cincinnati, Ohio: Writer's Digest Books, 1990. How to query successfully.

Dillard, Annie. *The Writing Life*. New York: Harper & Row, 1989. The everyday life of a writer, described with Dillard's characteristic immediacy and grace.

Elbow, Peter. *Embracing Contraries: Explorations in Learning and Teaching*. New York: Oxford, 1986. Essays on the nature of teaching and learning.

————. *Writing with Power: Techniques for Mastering the Writing Process*. New York: Oxford, 1981. Suggestions for discovering and exploring the writing process.

————. *Writing Without Teachers.* New York: Oxford, 1973. Practical advice for learning to write using the two-step creative process.

Else, Susan McBride. *Into the Deep: A Writer's Look at Creativity.* Portsmouth, N.H.: Heinemann, 1994. The author's insights into creativity, noted while working on a novel.

Field, Joanna. *A Life of One's Own.* 1936. Reprint. Los Angeles: J. P. Tarcher, 1981. Classic journey of self-exploration. Field, a pseudonym for an English psychoanalyst, searches for authenticity through a diary begun in 1926.

Forché, Carolyn. *The Country Between Us.* New York: Harper and Row, 1981. Poetry bearing witness to the people and politics of Latin America.

Friedman, Bonnie. *Writing Past Dark: Envy, Fear, Distraction, and Other Dilemmas in the Writer's Life.* New York: HarperPerennial, 1993. Friedman explores the darker side of the writer's life, offering wise and practical passage through this thorny maze ("How to learn faith? My friends taught me.")

Fry, Joan. "How-to Books for Writers: Who Needs 'Em?" *Poets & Writers Magazine.* March/April 1995, 39–49. A discussion of the value, for teachers and creative writers, of how-to books on writing. Includes a list of thirty-three writing books.

Fulton, Leon, ed. *The International Directory of Little Magazines and Small Presses.* Paradise, Calif.: Dustbooks, 1996. A reference book including addresses, type of material published, and submission guidelines.

Gage, Diane, and Marcia Coppess. *Get Published: Top Magazine Editors Tell You How.* New York: Henry Holt, 1994. Specific advice on content and submission, from the sources themselves.

Good Books for Writers

Gallwey, W. Timothy. *The Inner Game of Tennis.* Toronto, Canada: Bantam, 1974. Provides a theory and practice for teaching yourself to play tennis through Zen principles that applies to athletics, performance, and art more generally.

Gardner, John. *The Art of Fiction: Notes on Craft for Young Writers.* New York: Alfred A. Knopf, 1984. By now classic advice for the beginning writer.

———. *On Becoming a Novelist.* New York: Harper & Row, 1983. More on the writer's vocation.

Gere, Anne Ruggles. *Writing Groups: History, Theory, and Implications.* Carbondale: Southern Illinois University Press, 1987. The history and theory of writing groups in America.

Goldberg, Bonni. *Room to Write: Daily Invitations to a Writer's Life.* New York: Jeremy P. Tarcher/Putnam, 1996. Two hundred short studies—"doors"—into the places from which creative writing emerges: imagination, emotion, intellect, and soul.

Goldberg, Natalie. *Wild Mind.* New York: Bantam, 1990. Goldberg's second book of writing exercises, anecdotes, and inspiration about finding the "true source of creative power: the mind" and about living the writer's life.

———. *Writing Down the Bones: Freeing the Writer Within.* Boston: Shambhala, 1986. Writing exercises and comforting anecdotes generated from Goldberg's experiences as a student of Zen. Hailed by Judith Guest in 1986 as "simply the best aid and comfort around today."

Gordon, Karen Elizabeth. *The Transitive Vampire: A Handbook of Grammar for the Innocent, the Eager, and the Doomed.* New York: Times Books, 1984. A grammar book—not for the faint of heart.

Good Books for Writers

Guide to Literary Agents. Cincinnati, Ohio: Writer's Digest Books, 1996. All about agents, published yearly.

Hagen, Kay Leigh. *Internal Affairs: A Journalkeeping Workbook for Self-Intimacy.* New York: HarperSanFrancisco, 1990. An insightful guide to journal work.

Hogan, Linda. *Mean Spirit.* New York: Atheneum, 1990. A rich novel by an emerging writer.

Hoy, Nancy Jo. *The Power to Dream: Interviews with Women in the Creative Arts.* New York: Global City Press, 1995. Interviews with visual artists, writers, dancers, and musicians about their work.

Joselow, Beth Baruch. *Writing Without the Muse: 50 Beginning Exercises for the Creative Writer.* Brownsville, Ore.: Story Line Press, 1995. Useful exercises to help you start writing—with student examples.

Lamott, Anne. *Bird by Bird: Some Instructions on Writing and Life.* New York: Pantheon, 1994. Common sense advice ("short assignments," "shitty first drafts") told with Lamott's humor and insight ("Perfectionism is the voice of the oppressor, the enemy of the people").

Lanham, Richard A. *Revising Business Prose.* 3d ed. New York: Macmillan, 1987. Tough and to-the-point suggestions for revising any nonfiction writing.

Larson, Michael. *How to Write a Book Proposal.* Cincinnati, Ohio: Writer's Digest Books, 1985. Directions and examples, including a bibliography.

L'Engle, Madeleine. *A Circle of Quiet.* New York: Farrar, Straus & Giroux, 1972. One writer's attempt to find answers to the ultimate questions about her life.

Levoy, Gregg. *This Business of Writing.* Cincinnati, Ohio: Writer's Digest Books, 1992. A clear-sighted guide to the other side of the process.

Lipsett, Suzanne. *Surviving a Writer's Life.* New York: HarperSanFrancisco, 1994. Reflections on the experiences that made Lipsett a writer, offering writerly advice between the lines.

LMP (Literary Marketplace). New Providence, N.J.: R. R. Bowker, 1995. Directory of the American book publishing industry, from agents to presses to awards.

Macrorie, Ken. *Telling Writing.* 4th ed. Upper Montclair, N.J.: Boynton/Cook, 1985. A college textbook that encourages students to write tight active prose from personal experience, with exercises and precepts.

Mairs, Nancy. *Voice Lessons: On Becoming a (Woman) Writer.* Boston: Beacon, 1994. Essays on becoming a woman writer in Mairs's wonderfully personal voice.

Maisel, Eric. *Fearless Creating: A Step-by-Step Guide to Starting and Completing Your Work of Art.* New York: Putnam, 1995. Gives concrete advice on pushing back fear and resistance. For writers, visual artists, and performing artists.

McCarthy, Cormac. *All the Pretty Horses.* New York: Knopf, 1992. Sweeping novel by a wonderful craftsman of language.

McDaniel, Judith. *Sanctuary: A Journey.* Ithaca, N.Y.: Firebrand, 1987. A writer and activist explores the meaning of sanctuary in our lives.

Metzger, Deena. *Writing for Your Life: A Guide and Companion to the Inner Worlds.* New York: HarperSanFrancisco, 1992. A guide to personal creativity.

Miller, Casey, and Kate Swift. *The Handbook of Nonsexist Writing.* 2d ed. New York: Harper & Row, 1980. Essential guide to eradicating sexism in our language.

Murray, Donald. *Shoptalk: Learning to Write with Writers.* Portsmouth, N.H.: Boynton/Cook, 1990. A book of quotations, maxims, and advice on writing and writers edited by a noted writer and teacher.

———. *A Writer Teaches Writing.* 2d ed. Boston: Houghton

Mifflin, 1985. Advice from a well-known journalist and teacher.

Neff, Glenda Tennant, ed. *The Writer's Essential Desk Reference.* Cincinnati, Ohio: Writer's Digest Books, 1991. Complete survey of the writer's life, from health insurance and income tax to getting published.

Nelson, Victoria. *On Writer's Block: Removing the Barriers to Creativity.* Boston: Houghton Mifflin, 1993. How to let go of fear.

Newman, Lesléa. *Writing from the Heart: Inspiration and Exercises for Women Who Want to Write.* Freedom, Calif.: Crossing Press, 1993. Exercises for freewriting and other techniques of writing fiction.

Nhat Hanh, Thich. *Peace Is Every Step: The Path of Mindfulness in Everyday Life.* New York: Bantam Books, 1991. A Zen master and peace activist shows how to be mindful in our everyday activities.

Nin, Anaïs and Gunther Stuhlmann. *The Diary of Anaïs Nin.* New York: Swallow Press, 1966–1980. The revealing, and lengthy, diaries of a famous literary figure.

Novel and Short Story Writer's Market. Cincinnati, OH: Writer's Digest Books, 1996. A regularly published guide to the fiction market.

Oliver, Mary. *A Poetry Handbook.* New York: Harcourt Brace, 1994. A guide to writing poetry by a Pulitzer Prize-winning poet.

Olsen, Tillie. *Silences: Classic Essays on the Art of Creating.* New York: Delta/Seymour Lawrence, 1978. Drawing on many sources, Olsen explores the creative process and what derails it.

Paley, Grace. *Enormous Changes at the Last Minute: Stories.* New York: Farrar, Straus & Giroux, 1974. Collection of lively short fiction.

———. *The Little Disturbances of Man.* New York: Penguin, 1956. Innovative short works by one of the best.

Pearlman, Daniel D., and Paula R. Pearlman. *Guide to Rapid Revision*. 6th ed. Boston: Allyn & Bacon, 1996. Concise guide to correcting common writing problems.

Poet's Market. Cincinnati, OH: Writer's Digest Books, 1996. A regularly published guide to the poetry market.

Preston, Elizabeth; Monke, Ingrid; and Elizabeth Bickford. *Preparing Your Manuscript*. Boston: The Writer, 1986. Guidance in everything from grammar to copyright.

Prize Stories: The O. Henry Awards. New York: Doubleday, annual. Award-winning stories.

Rainer, Tristine. *The New Diary: How to Use a Journal for Self-Guidance and Expanded Creativity*. Los Angeles: J. P. Tarcher, 1978. Detailed suggestions for what kind of journal to keep and what to write there.

Rich, Adrienne. *What Is Found There: Notebooks on Poetry and Politics*. New York: W. W. Norton, 1993. The visionary poet reflects on poetry and politics in American life.

Rico, Gabriele Lusser. *Writing the Natural Way: Using Right-Brain Techniques to Release Your Expressive Powers*. Los Angeles: J. P. Tarcher, 1983. How to release your inner writer.

Russ, Joanna. *How to Suppress Women's Writing*. Austin: University of Texas Press, 1983. How women writers get blocked, written with humor.

Shapard, Robert, and James Thomas, eds. *Sudden Fiction: American Short-Short Stories*. Salt Lake City, Utah: G. M. Smith, 1986. A collection of one- to three-page masterpieces in short narrative.

———. *Sudden Fiction International: Sixty Short-Short Stories*.

New York: Norton, 1989. International short-short stories of note.

Shaughnessy, Susan. *Walking on Alligators: A Book of Meditations for Writers*. New York: HarperSanFrancisco, 1993. Page-by-page meditations, to be kept in a corner of your desk.

Stafford, William. *Writing the Australian Crawl: Views on the Writer's Vocation*. Ann Arbor: University of Michigan, 1978. Inspiration about writing, especially poetry.

Stegner, Wallace, with Edward Connery Lathem. *On the Teaching of Creative Writing: Responses to a Series of Questions*. Hanover, N.H.: Dartmouth College, 1988. Based on recorded discussions before a student audience, Stegner answers questions about creative writing.

Stein, Gertrude. *How to Write*. 1931. Reprint. Los Angeles: Sun & Moon Press, 1995. Stein's thoughts about the craft of writing, in her inimitable style.

Stern, Jerome. *Making Shapely Fiction*. New York: Laurel, 1991. Techniques used by fiction writers, in alphabetical order.

Sternberg, Janet, ed. *The Writer on Her Work: New Essays in New Territory*, vols. 1 and 2. New York: W. W. Norton, 1980 and 1991. Personal essays by women novelists, poets, and nonfiction writers.

Stone, Hal, and Sidra Stone. *Embracing Your Inner Critic: Turning Self-Criticism into a Creative Asset*. New York: HarperSanFrancisco, 1993. How to make your inner critic an ally, with exercises and examples.

Strunk, William, and E. B. White. *The Elements of Style*. 3d ed. New York: Macmillan, 1979. Presents "elementary rules of usage," "principles of composition," and "an approach to style" with Strunk's simplicity and White's beloved clarity.

Tibbetts, A. M. *To the Point: Efficient and Attractive Writing for Almost Any Audience.* Glenview, Ill.: Scott, Foresman, 1983. No-nonsense suggestions for clear writing.

Ueland, Brenda. *If You Want to Write: A Book About Art, Independence and Spirit.* 1938. Reprint. 2d ed. Saint Paul, MN: Graywolf, 1987. A classic on writing and creativity by a devotee of William Blake.

Walker, Alice. *In Search of Our Mothers' Gardens.* San Diego: Harcourt Brace, 1983. Essays by one of America's premier writers on writing, civil rights, and feminism.

Williams, Terry Tempest. *An Unspoken Hunger: Stories from the Field.* New York: Vintage, 1994. A naturalist and writer meditates on the place of wildness in our lives.

Woolf, Virginia. *A Writer's Diary: Being Extracts from the Diary of Virginia Woolf.* London: Hogarth Press, 1953. A quintessential writer's diary.

Writer's Market: Where and How to Sell What You Write. Cincinnati, Ohio: Writer's Digest Books, 1995. A guide to the market, published yearly.

Zinsser, William. *On Writing Well: An Informal Guide to Writing Nonfiction.* 5th ed. New York: HarperPerennial, 1994. Solid advice on the principles and methods for writing nonfiction from an elder statesman of writing. Also recommended are *Writing to Learn* and *Inventing the Truth: The Art and Craft of Memoir,* along with several other titles in the "Art and Craft of . . ." series edited by Zinsser.

Magazines:

The Writer
The Writer, Inc.
120 Boylston St.
Boston, MA 02116
(617) 423-3157

Other resources:

The Authors Guild, Inc.
330 W. 42nd St.
New York, NY 10036
(212) 563-5904

Good Books for Writers

Writer's Digest
F&W Publications
1507 Dana Ave.
Cincinnati, OH 45207
(513) 531-2222

Poets & Writers
Poets & Writers, Inc.
72 Spring St.
New York, NY 10012
(212) 226-3586

Writers Guild of America
East: 555 W. 57th St.
      New York, NY 10019
      (212) 245-6180
West: 8955 Beverly Blvd.
      W. Hollywood, CA
      90048
      (213) 550-1000

National Writers Union
13 Astor Place
New York, NY 10003
(212) 254-0279

PEN
Pen American Center
568 Broadway
New York, NY 10012
(212) 334-1660

Writer's Digest Books
1507 Dana Ave.
Cincinnati, OH 45207

Index

Agents, literary, 143–144, 197
All the Pretty Horses (McCarthy), 139
Allison, Dorothy, 71, 73
Anderson, Sherwood, 191
"Appetite" (prompt), 108–110
Art of Fiction, The (Gardner), 21
Artist's Way, The (Cameron), 12, 133, 193
Artistic considerations, 41–45
  common interests of members, 42–45
  experience and commitment of members, differences in, 42–43
  genre differences, 43–44, 56
Atlantic Monthly, The, 194
Attendance, 148–153
  changing meeting night, 152–153
  importance of core members, 153
  effect on group, 151–153
  effect on individual writer, 148–151
  erratic, 46, 151, 177–178
  "Group Check-in" exercise, 152
  low, 51, 148, 172, 173
  meet less often for greater attendance, 153
  "must show" policies, 153
Attention, importance of paying, 21, 26–28, 65, 110
  to self as one reads aloud, 123
Atwood, Margaret, 111, 140
Audience, 7, 8, 24–26, 32, 36
Author, role of during a critique, 126
  avoiding self-explanation, 127
  define what you want, 122, 126–127
  experience during reading aloud, 123–124
  guiding discussion of work, 125, 129
  silence during traditional critique, 14–15, 129
Autobiography, 29, 30, 117, 184

Bastard Out of Carolina (Allison), 71
Becoming a Writer (Brande), 16, 33, 192
Belles Lettres, 194
Bernays, Anne, 193
Berrigan, Ted, 14
Best American Essays, 194

Best American Poetry, 194
Best American Short Stories, 194
Beth, 4, 25, 27–28, 31, 72, 96, 105–06, 183–84
Bird by Bird (Lamott), 134, 193
Block. *See* Writer's block
Bly, Robert, 14
Books, good for writers, 203–213
Bowles, Jane, 104
Brain
  left hemisphere, 19
  logical side, 17
  right hemisphere, 19
Brand, Alice G., 17
Brande, Dorothea, 16, 33, 192, 193
Brennan, Karen, 140
Burroway, Janet, 21, 130
Business, of writing, 199

Cameron, Julia, 12, 133, 193
Carver, Raymond, 14
Change, staying open to, 147–148, 173–181
Characters, working with as prompt, 103–107
  prompts in a bag, 113–116
  "What's in a Name?" 104–107
  writing each other's, 117
"Check-in, Group," exercise, 152, 163, 169
Children's Writer's and Illustrator's Market, 196
"China" (prompt), 67–69
Classes and workshops, 10, 39, 194–195
Collaboration, 85, 107–118, 173, 180
  of writing minds, 77
Collective energy, 23–24, 32
Colleges and universities, for classes, 39, 194–195
Colors, writing from as prompt, 100–103
Commitment, 37, 42–43, 56
  faltering, 153
  to group, 146, 151, 162, 166, 179, 180
  to self as writer, 25, 32

Index

to writing, 150, 151
Community of writers, xvi, 12, 137, 194, 200
Comparison, 154, 160–161
Competitiveness and jealousy, 31, 61, 147, 160–161, 172
  and comparison, 200
  lack of in group, 29
Concentration, 17
Conflict
  in group, 147–148, 163–166
  over own writing, 147–148
Contests, literary, 198
Continuity between meetings, 190
Control, giving up, 28
Core group issues, 35, 55–56, 146
  "Core group issues" exercise, 55–56
Country Between Us, The (Forche), 182
Craft
  books on, 21
  issues of, 132
  honing, 15, 37
Creative process, 14, 15, 18, 19. *See also* Writing process
  organic, 16
  two–step process, 16, 17–19
Creative writing programs. *See* Writing programs, academic
Creativity, 17–19, 192
Critical mind, 18–19, 20, 32
  silencing, 20, 31
Critical model, 14–15
  traditional workshop model, 14–15, 129
Critical skills, 38
Criticism, 11, 37
  avoiding negative, 123, 125
  excessive, 6, 128–129
  of self, 18, 19, 31–32, 154–156
  sensitivity to, 158
Critiques, using readers', 186–187
Critiquing, 62–63, 120, 126–131. *See also* Feedback *and* Responding to writing
  be specific, 158
  debate among respondents, 159
  fiction, 129–130
  issues to consider, 62–63
  nonfiction, 131
  professional, 194–195
  rules for effective, 126–131
  troubleshooting, 156–159
    honesty in critiquing, 158–159
    "It's Not Ready Yet" syndrome, 157

"right" vs. "wrong" mode, 159
Cuevas, Gertrude Eastman, 104
Cutout images (prompt), 95–98

Daphne, 27–28, 30, 74–76, 115
Dawn, 2–3, 26–27, 28, 30, 79–81, 86–87, 89, 91, 92, 103–04, 108, 109–10, 116, 183
"Defining Individual Needs" exercise, 57
DeLillo, Don, 96
Descriptive language, 113, 114, 115–117
"Design mind," 19. *See also* Brain, right hemisphere
"Desire" (prompt), 34
Dialogue (in a story), 45, 117
Dialogue, as response to a prompt, 98
"Dialogue, Internal," exercise, 155–156
Dillard, Annie, 1
Discipline, 17, 25, 37
Discouragement, 9, 23, 30
Discussion, 10, 61–62, 131–145
Drafts, 16, 141, 157
Drawing, 90–95
Dreams, 190
  as prompt, 99

Editing, 16, 21, 33
  premature, 19
Editors, 34, 144, 196
Effort, dangers of continual willful, 17
Elbow, Peter, 16–21
Elements of Style, The (Strunk and White), 21
Eliot, T. S., xvi
Emotion vs. intellect, in draft, 17
Emotional power in writing, 27–28, 38, 184
Ending a group, 172–173
Enormous Changes at the Last Minute (Paley), 140
Exchanging notebooks (prompt), 107–110
"Exchanging Work for the First Time" exercise, 58
Exercises, writing (guide to group), 201–202
Exhaustion, 149
  overcoming, 23
Experimenting, 29–30, 32, 38, 144–145, 148
"Exploring the Writing Process" exercise, 59

216

Index

Faulkner, William, 138
Family responsibilities, 147, 149, 166–167, 173, 182, 188
"Fathers" (prompt), 33, 67
Fear, xv, xvi, 7, 26
   of exposure, 26, 31, 155–156
   of reading aloud, 61
   of sharing work, 36, 155
   of writing, xv, 132–137
   of writing the truth, 34–35
   of writing together, 30–32
Feedback, xvii, 9, 13, 156, 179, 180, 186. *See also* Responding to writing *and* Critiquing
   at all stages of writing process, 157
   erratic, 151–152
   honesty in, 158–159
   immediate, 118
   in-depth on portfolios, 173
   rules of engagement, 121–122
Fiction, 29–30, 43, 79, 117
   critiquing, questions to ask, 129–130
   guides to writing, 21
   writers in groups, 44
Fine arts. *See* Writing programs, academic
First group meeting, 7, 52–57
Flexibility, 52–54, 146, 148, 173, 180
"Flying—Porter Pond" (painting), 95
Food, 48, 50
Forche, Carolyn, 182
Form (in writing), 26, 29, 117
Four elements (prompt), 1, 78–82, 183
Fragments, of writing, 29, 82, 184
   connecting to longer work, 29, 126
   what are they? 139–140
   what to do with them? 158–159
Franklin, Benjamin, 12–13
Freewriting, 1, 19–21, 22–23, 70, 120, 171
   benefits of, 19–21
   connecting with work done at home, 176, 178
   cut through left-brain activity, 22–23
   definition of, 1, 19
   no rules, 70
   responses to, 124–126
   theory of, 15–20, 25
Friedman, Bonnie, 191, 192

Gallwey, W. Timothy, 65
Gardner, John, 14, 21
Gender, of members, 47–48

Generative writing, 15, 18, 20, 21, 24, 36, 38
Genre, 41, 195
   considerations for group, 43–44, 56
Gentl, Andrea, 95
Gere, Anne Ruggles, 12, 13
"Getting Dirty" (short story), 183
Godwin, Gail, 14
Gone with the Wind (Mitchell), 197
Grand Street, 194
Granta, 194
"Group Check-in" exercise, 152, 163, 169
Guide to Literary Agents, 197

Hagen, Kay Leigh, 190
"Hair" (prompt), 67, 132
Harpers, 194
Havendish, Temple (character), 104, 107
Hogan, Linda, 104
"Home" (prompt), 67, 70–71
Honesty, 56
   in critiquing, 128, 158–159
   in discussing group issues, 165
   key element in successful group, 146, 180
"How Do I Know I'm a Writer?" 140–141
"How Do I Know What This Piece of Writing Is and What Do I Do with It?," 139–140
How to Write a Book Proposal (Larson), 197
How to Write Irresistible Query Letters (Cool), 197
Howard, Jane, 14

"I kissed a _____ once" (prompt), 27, 74–76
"Ideal Writing Group" exercise, 54–56
If You Want to Write (Ueland), 16, 17, 24, 192
Imagery, working with as prompt, 89–103
Images, 21
   as beginning to story, 4, 22, 89–90
   cutouts (prompt), 95–98
Imagination, need for "moodling," 17
Impromptu prompts, 74–78
In Search of Our Mothers' Gardens (Walker), 146
Inner Game of Tennis, The (Gallwey), 65
Insecurity, 60, 168, 171
Isolation, 12

Index

Inspiration, 12, 188, 193
  from others, 30
Intellect vs. emotion, in draft, 17
Intention, importance of giving up, 28–29
Internal Affairs (Hagen), 190
"Internal Dialogue" exercise, 155–156
Intuition, trusting, 28, 29, 132
Invention. *See* Generative writing
Iowa Writers' Workshop. *See* University of Iowa Writers' Workshop
Irving, John, 14
Isolation, xv, 12, 200
  breaking out of, 26

Jackie N., 92, 168–69
Jacqueline, 29, 30, 37, 38, 44, 69, 83, 87, 92, 93, 101, 140, 184
Jealousy and competitiveness, 160–161
Jo Anne, 31, 70, 73, 108, 109, 172
Journal, 11
  personal, 189
  process, 45
  writer's, 189–181
Judgment, withholding, 20–21, 25, 29, 61, 188
Justice, Donald, 14

Kincaid, Jamaica, 138
Kumin, Maxine, 198

Lamott, Anne, 134, 193
Landscape of the soul (prompt), 90–95, 171
Laughter, 8, 136, 148, 161, 162
Leadership issues, 50–52, 161–163
  designated leader, 162–163
  dominant leader, 161–162
  lack of, 51, 162, 163
  "Leadership Play" exercise, 162
  problems with, 161–163
  rotating, 52, 163
  unwilling leader, 161–165
Leaving a group, 172–173
LeCarre, John, 197
Levine, Philip, 14
Levoy, Gregg, 199
Library, 39, 49, 142, 169, 193, 194, 195, 196, 197
Lickin, April Mae (character), 106–107
Lipsett, Suzanne, 192, 198
Listening
  active, 125–126
  loss of, 178

well, 8, 123–126, 148
List of words (as prompt), 82–85
  list based on "mountain" (prompt), 176
Literary Marketplace (*LMP*), 196
Little Disturbances of Man, The (Paley), 140
Longer pieces of writing, 118–119, 126, 147, 176
Looping, 178

Macrorie, Ken, 16
Magazines for writers, 213
Magnetic Poetry Kit^R (prompt), 85–89
Mairs, Nancy, 7, 123
"Mara Floating" (painting), 95
Market, literary, 25, 195–197
  appropriate, 197
McCarthy, Cormac, 139
Mean Spirit (Hogan), 104
Meetings, how to structure, 52–63
  being open, 52–54
  critiquing drafts, 62–63
  first meeting, 52–57
  response and discussion, 61–62
  second through fourth meetings, 57–63
  writing together, 60–61
Membership
  advertising for, 40
  changes, 167–172, 180
    dropping out, 171–172
    gaining members, 168–171
    welcoming new members, 169–171
  common interests, 44–45
  domination by a few, 164
  experience and commitment, differences in, 42–43
  finding other group members, 39–40, 40–42
  gender considerations, 47–48
  new member, benefits of, 170
  number of members, 46
  requirements, 46–47
Memoir, 43
MFA (Master of Fine Arts) programs. *See* Writing programs, academic
Mindfulness, 65–66
Moody, Rick, 138
Morphing the group, 178
"Mountain," list of words from (prompt), 176
Mourning, Alonzo, 104
Murder in the Dark (Atwood), 140

Index

Murray, Donald, 16
"My relationship with Carl" (prompt), 177
My Sister's Hand in Mine (Bowles), 104

Nabokov, Vladimir, 197
Needs, as writers, 11, 15, 35–39, 54–55, 172, 179
  change over time, 147
  "Defining Individual Needs" exercise, 57
New Diary, The (Rainer), 190
New York Review of Books, 194
New York Times Book Review, 194
New Yorker, The, 194
Nhat Hahn, Thich, 65
Nicky, 24, 30–31
Nin, Anaïs, 190
Nonfiction, 43, 56
  critiquing, questions to ask, 131
  submission for publication, 143
Notebooks, passing (prompt), 107–110
Novel, submission for publication, 143, 196–197
Novel and Short Story Writer's Market, 196

O'Connor, Flannery, 14
Oliver, Mary, 21
On Writing Well (Zinsser), 21
Organizational details, 42, 46–52
  gender of members, 47–48
  leadership issues, 50–52
  how long to meet, 49–50
  membership requirements, 46–47
  number of members, 46
  scheduling in advance, 49–50
  when to meet, 49–50
  where to meet, 48–49

Painter, Pamela, 193
Paley, Grace, 140
Participation in group, reluctance to, 153–156
  fear of exposure, 155–156
  "Internal Dialogue" exercise, 154, 155–156
  low self-confidence, 154–155
  writing group is not a class, 154
Passing notebooks (prompt), 107–110
Peace Is Every Step (Nhat Hahn), 65
Perfectionism, 157
Personal issues
  conflict between members, 163–166
  dominant member, 164

Phillips, Jayne Anne, 14, 138
Pick-Up Sticks or spontaneous sentences (prompt), 110–113
Pima Writers' Workshop, 198
Playwriting, 45
Plot (in a story), 29, 89, 108, 117, 130
Ploughshares, 194
Poet's Market, 196
Poetry, 43–44, 82–84, 89, 96, 97, 98, 117, 140
  Daphne's, 27–28, 74–76
  poets-only group, 44
  traditional critique, 14
  guide for writing, 21
Poets and Writers (organization), 193, 213
Poets and Writers, 193, 195, 213
Poetry Handbook, The (Oliver), 21
Premise for writing, 74–78
Prize Stories: The O. Henry Awards, 194
Process. *See* Creative process *and* Writing process
Process journal (exercise), 45
Process vs. product, 9, 38, 58, 66
Product vs. process, 9, 38, 58, 66
Prompts, 22, 65–119
  collaboration, 107–118
    characters, 117
    new style, 117–118
    passing notebooks, 107–110
    prompts in a bag, 113–117
    spontaneous sentences, 110–113
  definition of, 22
  seek new, 66–67
  sustaining longer works, 118–119
  using writing from group, 183–186
  working with characters, xvi, 103–107
    prompts in a bag, 113–116
    what's in a name? 104–107
    writing someone else's characters, 117
  working with imagery, xvii, 89–103
    colors, 100–103
    cutout images, 95–98
    dreams, 99
    landscape of the soul, xvii, 90–95
  working with words, xvii, 67–89
    four elements, xvii, 1, 78–82
    impromptu prompts, 74–78
    list, 82–85
    Magnetic Poetry Kit®, 85–89
    sentences, 71–78
    words, 67–71
Proposal, book, 197

Index

Protected writing time, xvi, 149, 189
Publication, 10, 37, 142–144, 160, 161, 186, 189, 195–198. *See also* Submitting work for publication
reason not to join group, 10
Published work
as models, 59–60, 169
reading, 45, 59–60, 169
Publishers, directory for, 195–196
Publishers Weekly, 196
Pushcart Press, 197

Query letter, 197

Rainer, Tristine, 190
Reading books, 10, 11, 192–194
Readings, literary, 10, 194
Reading work aloud
excerpts written outside group, 125
fear of, 60–61, 154
for playwrights and screenwriters, 45
freewriting, 2, 25–26, 27, 120, 126
intimidation, 30–32
listening to own language, 25–26, 27
need for, 155
"Real" writer, 36
"Real" writing, 20, 29
Rejection, from publisher, 148, 154, 160, 197–198
Relaxation, importance of, 17
Resources for writers, 213–214
Respondent, responsibilities of
be honest, 128
be specific, 127–128
honor author's feelings, 128
identify what is working, 127
speak right after reading, 127
Responding to writing, 61–62, 120–131. *See also* Critiquing *and* Feedback
author's participation, 122, 125–127
continuum of techniques, 122–131
formal critique of work written outside group, 126–131
responding to freewriting, 124–126
how to begin, 120–123
marking drafts, 121–122
respondent's role, 127–129
Retreat, 118, 173–180, 195
collective with other groups, 180
regular part of group, 179

Revision, 16, 18, 21, 36, 62, 119, 157, 178, 185
how to use writing from the group, 183–186, 186–187
Rich, Adrienne, 200
Rico, Gabriele Lusser, 18
Risk, 11, 26–28, 52, 128, 155
in responding, 128
Rotten Rejections (Bernard), 197

Safety, in writing group, 123
Saturday Review, 194
Scene (in writing), 21, 29, 61
Scheduling. *See* Writing group
Screenwriting, 45
Seattle Writers Club (1903), 13
Self-confidence, low, 154–155
Sentences (prompt), 71–78
impromptu (prompt), 74–78
"Sequoia" (color prompt), 101–102
Sewanee Review, 194
"Sharing Writing Models" exercise, 59–60
Shaughnessy, Susan, 193
Short stories, 29, 89, 140
submission for publication, 142–144
traditional critique, 14
"Shrines" (prompt), 27, 183–184
"Shut up, Joe" (prompt), 177
"Sign mind," 19. *See also* Brain, left hemisphere
Silence, in group, 30–32, 147. *See also* Participation in group, reluctance to
Specificity, need for, 139, 158, 165
Snodgrass, W. D., 14
Speaking up, 131–144
Stafford, William, 14
Standards, traditional, 10, 21, 37–38
"Statues," list of words from (prompt), 82–84
Stegner, Wallace, 14
Stein, Gertrude, 12
Strand, Mark, 14
Strunk, William, Jr., 21
Style, choose a new (prompt), 117–118
Submitting work for publication, 36, 142–144, 195–199
appropriate journals, 161, 162, 198, 227
advantage of personal contact, 143–144
literary agents, 143–144
multiple submissions, 197

Index

on a regular basis, 143, 197
preferred manner of submission, 197
process, 142–144
sending out a selection of work, 143
single-mindedness, 196
submission fest, 173–174
Sudden Fiction (Shapard and Thomas), 140
Surviving a Writer's Life (Lipsett), 192, 198
Susan N., 5, 23, 24, 29, 31, 68, 72, 84, 91, 92, 93–94, 102–03, 106–07, 108–09
Susan R., 3–4, 23, 29, 30, 70–71, 72–73, 88, 97–98, 114–15,139–40
Sustaining longer works (prompt), 118–119
Synergy in group, 23, 41, 147

Talking writing, 120–145. *See also* Discussion
Tate, James, 14
Teaching writing, 15–16
Theories of writing. *See* Writing, theories of
Time
  conflict with families, 166–167
  conflict with scheduling, 147, 149, 151
  protected writing, xvi, 149, 189
  regularly scheduled writing, 9, 187
Transformation, xvii, 7, 11, 12–32
Trust
  need for, 146–148, 164
  lack of, 147
Truth, 200
  finding your own, 34–35
Tucson writing group, xvi–xvii, 6–7
  first meeting, 7, 33
  members, xvi
  retreat, 173–180
  typical meeting, 1

Ueland, Brenda, 16, 17, 24, 192
University of Arizona, 6, 148
  English Department, 168
  Extended University, 47–48, 132
University of Iowa Writers' Workshop, 14
  graduates of, 14

"Video" (short story), 96
Voice, 117, 137–139
  definition of, 137

inner, 6, 198
  trusting own, xvi, 26
Voice (in a story), 137–138
Voice Lessons: On Becoming a (Woman) Writer (Mairs), 7
Von Duyn, Mona, 14

Wake Up and Live (Brande), 193
Wakefield, Dan, 14
Walker, Alice, 146
Walking on Alligators (Shaughnessy), 193
What If? (Bernays and Painter), 193
What's in a name? (prompt), 104–107
White, E. B., 21
Wideman, John Edgar, 14
Wild Dreams (Brennan), 140
WILLA (Women in Life and Literature Assembly), 183
Williams, Tennessee, 14
Winesburg, Ohio (Anderson), 191
Women-only groups, 48
Women's Review of Books, The, 194
Woolf, Virginia, xvi, 120
Words, working with a prompt, 67–89
  words, single, as prompt, 67–71
Workshops, writing, 9, 194–195
  model for critiquing, 14–15, 129–131
Writer
  beginning, 42
  definition of, 140–141
  development of, 32
  experienced, 42
  hard to be one, 150
  "real" writer, 36, 147, 191
  surviving as one, 147
  treating self as one, 191
  working, 197
Writer, The, 193, 213
Writer's block, 10, 34, 36, 41, 132–137, 147–148, 151
  leading to insight, 132–137
  natural occurrence, 32
  strategies for overcoming, 134, 136–137
  "Writer's Block Metaphors" exercise, 135–136
Writer's Diary, A (Woolf), 120
Writer's Digest, 193, 213
Writer's Digest Books, 196, 214
Writer's Market, 196
Writing
  as personal act, 12
  as private act, 12, 31

Index

basic guidelines, 21, 194–195
business of, 199
changes in, 200
focus on in group, 148, 165
life beyond writing group, 182–200
lonely task, xvi
partner, 192
practice, 65–67, 185
"real," 20
self, 7
space, 188
steady rhythm of, 185
theories of, 15–19
time, protected, xvi–xvii, 149, 189
time, regularly scheduled, 9, 141, 187–188
together, 12, 22–32, 60–61, 66, 177
Writing Fiction (Burroway), 21, 130
Writing group
  artistic concerns, 42–45
  attendance, 148–153
  audience, 24–26
  beginning of, 33–64
  benefits of, 7–10
  change, staying open to, 173–181
  collective energy, 23–24
  conflict in, 163–166
  core issues, 35, 55–56, 146
  exposing raw writing, 26, 31
  family responsibilities, 195–197
  flexibility, 52–54, 146, 148, 173, 180
  "Ideal Writing Group" exercise, 54–56
  interpersonal issues, 163–166
  jealousy and competitiveness, 160–161
  key elements, 146
  leadership, 50–52, 161–163
  leaving or ending a group, 172–173
  life beyond, 182–200
  membership changes, 167–172
  "mutual improvement" groups, 12
  organizational concerns, 35, 46–52
  process, sharing, 9–10

reasons to join, 7–10, 169
reasons to skip, 149–150
regular time for, 9, 187–188
reluctance to participate, 153–156
retreat, 173–180
scheduling meeting times, 49–51, 56
stock images of, 36
structure of, 52–64
sustaining over the long haul, 146–181
talking writing, 10
troubleshooting critiquing sessions, 156–159
wrong reasons to join, 10–11
Writing Groups: History, Theory, and Implications (Gere), 12
Writing Life, The (Dillard), 1
Writing model
  "Sharing Writing Models" exercise, 59–60
  traditional, 16, 129
Writing Past Dark (Friedman), 191, 192
Writing process, 9–10, 16, 18, 21, 34, 37, 132, 141, 184, 185–186
  different for each person, 22
  "Exploring the Writing Process" exercise, 59
  sharing, 9–10, 144–145
Writing programs, academic, 6–7, 14–15, 37, 44, 120, 128, 129, 195
Writing prompts. *See* Prompts
Writing the Natural Way (Rico), 18–19
Writing together, 12–32, 60–61, 120, 177
  collective energy, 23–24
  learn better to write alone, 23
  what happens during, 22–32
Writing with Power (Elbow), 17–18
Writing Without Teachers (Elbow), 16, 19
Writing workshops, 14, 39
  traditional model, 14–15, 36, 129

Zinsser, William, 21

About the Authors

Dawn Denham Haines received a B.M. from Eastman School of Music, and is a doctoral candidate in Rhetoric, Composition and the Teaching of English at the University of Arizona, where she teaches first-year composition.

Susan Newcomer has a B.A. in English from Wellesley College and an M.A. in English Literature from Rutgers University. She has edited books and journals in Seattle, New York, London, and Tucson. She currently teaches in the composition program at the University of Arizona. She is cofounder of the writing group.

Jacqueline Raphael received a B.A. in English from Yale University and an M.F.A. in creative writing from the University of Arizona. In Tucson, she teaches poetry and writing to children and composition and creative writing to adults. She recently coauthored a book on innovative exams in college-level science and has contributed, as editor or writer, to other articles and books about education.